NEW GENERATION BEATS 2024 ANTHOLOGY

NATIONAL BEAT POETRY FOUNDATION, INC.

Published by
New Generation Beat Publications

ISBN: 978-1-957654-19-5

Debbie Tosun Kilday - Editing & Cover Design.

Human Error Publishing - Editing & Formatting

The 2024 New Generation Beats Anthology

Is dedicated to the memory of Andy Clausen, Lifetime Beat Poet Laureate who passed away on April 11, 2024 at the age of 80. But he was so much more important than his title. He was an inspiration to writers everywhere. He taught us to not be afraid to speak your truth. He taught us to embrace life with all your might, because some day that life will be taken from you.

Andy believed in living and he did so with a passion. When I first met him and the love of his life, Pamela Twining in 2020, Andy and Pamela traveled from their home in Woodstock, NY to meet me in CT at my annual Beat Poetry Festival. Upon meeting me Andy said, "You know Deb, at first I wasn't sure about you and wondered why you started this organization. But now that I have met you and all the other people here, I'm so happy to find there are still real and good people in this world. Thank you for keeping the beat alive.

Andy was one of the original beat generation of writers. Although he wasn't as well known as Allen Ginsberg, or Gregory Corso, he was an important voice that we should all remember and try to emulate with our own writing.

I've made it my mission to continue the legacy of the original beat generation, but to evolve into the future with a new generation of beat writers, not afraid to write about things that matter and to not be silenced.

TABLE OF CONTENTS

Kim Acrylic - He Burns

My phantoms nebulize in the wake of sand storms
in the shape of religion.

I feast with scalloped emotions which are
only fit for the mundane minded.

I liquify insults to turn them into thick,
pink kisses upon my blazing spine.

My human shaped temple
burns like a thousand witches dancing at the stake.

Sour tears drench my hair as if the rains
have been baptized in acidic beliefs.

Manic constellations forge unwilling
signatures for death and oblivion.

The bright noise of the muted plague shakes
pity off those deceased.

Ailing, crooked fingers draw monsters
in the sand creating a homemade God.

I fall to the beat of the echo that replays
the heartbeat that ceased at your birth.

You speak with an arrhythmia
only well known to broken legends and hearts.

Gluttons with breast milk dripping
from their mouths scream blasphemous lullabies.

Feet broken, eyes sewn, you grace
the morose lands with a quiet little hell.

Kim Acrylic has been writing poetry for over 30 years. Her contribution in the community is vast. Her work has been in several anthologies alongside the likes of IAMX, Sadie Frost, Michael Madsen, Charlie Sheen, even collaborating post death with Andy Warhol. She just released a new volume of poetry “My Pink Skull”

Michael D. Amitin - Song for Isaackito

He's a man of music
delivering joy to faraway places
villages spaces filled with children, grateful mothers
showering him with gifts, candies all things for a brother

A magi's two-step dream he stumbles upon
artists of wonder on yonder-lit African streets
records them remotely, Issackito's music scene

Then the music stopped
Jihad Joe came with his monkey wrench
yelled 'turn it off'
"you play this secular music
and you'll carry your head home"
like St Denis on a Martyr's mountain

Women dancing freely now at the point of a knife
stumbling dark fog mantras
is this the liberation we want?

Liquid band wagoneers smoking 3am fears
in brainwashed kumbaya jugendbund beer camps
stoking Joe's weird trance

As his ignoble kings grind the dust of misery
in cloakroom deserts far removed from battle scar seams
hiding in rich summer shadows, puff-chested mantles
puffing smoke to the song of a son's early grave

While across the sea
sweet lipped missionaries peddle their
open-your wallet ballet

Why can't we just let people be
figure out for themselves how to navigate fragile humanity

Isaackito smiles, he's still got the beat
somewhere in a dark village night- sounds of silence,
crunching leaves

footsteps creep candlelight prayer night windows

No one can shut down
what's been there since the earth was round
sound is god, vibrations travel

Michael D. Amitin, poet, musician, originally from Los Angeles, now lives in Paris. Honored as International Beat Poet Laureate 2020-2021, his work has been published in Poetry Pacific, California Quarterly, North of Oxford, Love Love Magazine, Paris Lit Up, The Dreaming Machine and others. A poetic collaboration with Parisian Photographer Julie Peiffer can be found on fb Riverlights, and many of Amitin's poems can be read at the instagram site bearing his name.

Susan Kay Anderson - In a Way

1.
The town was more
and the marsh a dangerous place
neon orange much needed to be seen by hunters
through the bristled cattails, no thank you
just to sink into the muck. I thought no way
even driving past was precariously inter-stellar.

What sort of pedestrians
careless in crossing through slow motion engines
creaking with too much and the train whistles sound only
long
in the town with tracks along the river
fields and brambles.

In town I reassessed my thinking
all feeling shoved aside into Nature's Pantry
where I wandered the too-small aisles
with nothing in my basket but soap and candles.

If anyone could solve
what signs had been erased
even searching for the nearest mini-mall
somewhere to hang out and bide my time
was a chore soon forgotten along the highway
that led up to mountains.

2.
When I returned I disappeared more and more each return
to indoor dim lighting stale air dull carpet thuds and dishes
closest when I was a housecleaner in the swanky beach lots.
The time in outskirts of Denver cul-de-sacs nothing again
endless round and rounds locating a library before closing
hours then backto a basement apartment I barely escaped
each time (the huge blue couch) each place took no getting
used to no adjustment in those days of how/knowhow,
intrinsic mining down into reserves inside mountains.

3.
On my resume trying too hard
Forest Service and Bureau of Land Management stints
into wildernesses still in my every step
those various reports tucked under my fingernails,
knee joints
ankle bites, mosquitos, poison oak rashes, sweat
abrasions, blisters.

Susan Kay Anderson lives in southwestern Oregon's Umpqua River Basin. Her long poem "Man's West Once" was selected for Barrow Street Journal's "4 X 2 Project" and is included in Mezzanine (2019). Anderson also published Virginia Brautigan Aste's memoir, Please Plant This Book Coast To Coast (2021). https://www.pw.org/directory/writers/susan_kay_anderson

Martin Appleby - Knock Off Bukowski

I wanted to write a funny poem
about ChatGPT
my plan was to ask it
to write a poem
in the style of Martin Appleby
and hope that it would
not have a clue
who I was

but it did
though the poem it wrote
titled "Night Shift Epiphany"
read more like
knock off Bukowski
than Martin Appleby

maybe it didn't
really know who I was
after all
or maybe I am
just a knock off Bukowski.

Martin Appleby is a punk, poet, vegetarian, cider drinking scumbag from Hastings, England. He edits Paper and Ink Literary Zine and runs Scumbag Press.

Dr. Santosh Bakaya - The Silent Voice

I have many voices I know; how many do you have?
Two? Three? four?
I can howl. Can you howl too?
I can growl. Can you growl too? My voice can sway.
It can pirouette and dance. It can even sashay.
My voice can sneer, wring a tear;
it can prowl- cry foul! It can scold and berate.
It has the power to indict modern ways.
But why this suffocation?
Why can my voice not rise to the occasion?
Why can't it become a celebration of every living being?

Ginsberg howled in 112 lines- spontaneous, wild, raw, and
untethered.
But, why do I feel like The Little Mute Boy of Frederico Lorca?
Can't even howl two lines of dissent.
I seethe at the world's higgledy-piggeldy confusion.
Wring my hands in helpless rage at its capacity for mendacity.
But why am I afraid to put words on paper in profusion?
They try to manipulate my voice, asking me to conform.
Has my voice also been held captive by the King of

Crickets?
But that is unfair, is it not? Where is my right to
self-expression?
Do we have, "no more to say and nothing to weep for?" *1
I hear the guns of war, can they not be silenced like my voice?
Can they not be held captive by the enigmatic King of the
Crickets?*

*1 Ginsberg: Kaddish for Naomi
*2 Frederico Garcia Lorca: The Little Mute Boy

Dr. Santosh Bakaya - Internationally acclaimed for her poetic biography of Mahatma Gandhi, *Ballad of Bapu*,and another biography of Martin Luther King Jr. *Only in Darkness Can You See the Stars.* Dr. Bakaya is an academic, poet, biographer, novelist, short-story writer, Ted X speaker, critic, and creative writing mentor, who has participated in many Poetry Festivals.

Her Ted Talk on the Myth of Writers Block is very popular in creative writing circles.

She has written 28 very well-received books across different genres.

Tohm Bakelas - surprise

For two nights you tried
photographing the rain.
All your efforts proved
futile. Each picture was
blurred and dull, a grey
mess of weak shadows.
This is hard evidence of
the injustice of experience.
Rather than embracing
the rain, you tried to
capture it. Rather than
enjoying the moment,
you tried to document
it. You, a poet, should
know better than to
meddle into worlds
unknown. Laughing at
the irony of the situation,
your breath floats like
a pale ghost through the
black night. You wonder
if anyone else sees this,
if anyone else is alive.
You strike a match
in the cold dark,
surprise: you're
alone.

Tohm Bakelas is a social worker in a psychiatric hospital. He was born in New Jersey, resides there, and will die there. He is the author of several collections of poetry, including "Cleaning the Gutters of Hell" (Zeitgeist Press, 2023) and "The Ants Crawl in Circles" (Bone Machine, Inc., 2024).

Randy Barnes - Unfinished Business

In droves the neo-whatevers do the cliff-walk
side arms on alert a romantic duck and dive
identity extrapolation comes in colors
red for neck white for race blue for mood
creatures insulated and isolated in defiant plumage
real results in make-believe digression
fed with images the menu strikes a chord
thought transfer the big guess assault
the painted skeptic a patchwork of ransomed clarity
what passes gives nobility to witless obsession
and yes words warrant the charm of failure
focus understood as a massive so-what
aliens each to another in rhetorical squalor
traffic constitutes attention and bodies as money
fuck the audience good they'll bleed for the cause
spectacle's another day at the beach
and entertainment's the grand sedative that's just too hard to beat.

Randy Barnes lives and works in the foothills of the Olympic and Cascade mountain ranges of western Washington. He has published extensively both nationally and internationally with two books of poetry to be published in the near future. He was awarded a Lifetime Historian Beat Poet Laureate from the NBF in 2020.

James Barr - Song of the Dust Devil

East Texas specter.
Centered in your robe of dust.
Full moon, azure sky.
A white, brahma bull
Unmoved by your fine, ochre sash
Beneath its willow.
Pure tranquillo,
Fragranced by mesquite and citrus groves.
The whispers of your secrets
As fleeting as your dance.

James Barr is editor of New Rotvrier Review poetry magazine, based out of Upstate, South Carolina. He is dedicated to the promotion and preservation of rotvrier poetry, a collaborative, syncretic aesthetic evolution currently underway.

Carlos Barrera - Gotham

This town used to be like Gotham
Filled with crime
And sin
And losers
And the bars were always open
For its dreamers
And its boozers.

For its novelists & jokers
For the wise men
Passing by
Every dream once told a story
Every truth
Once told a lie.

Every corner had a smile
From brown skinned blon' marvelettes
There was once
A place for actors
Debutantes
And vedettes.

Negligees
And stilettos
Worn by angels in disguise
Thorny crowns
And neon halos
Worn by devils in demise.

Every square had hobo prophets
Warning
'Bout the end of times
While the midnight lonesome poets
Tried
To find the perfect rhymes.

In a town
That was like Gotham
Built on blood & stolen land

You could look out
For redemption
It was always there…
At hand…

Carlos Barrera is a writer & librarian from San Antonio, Texas. Most of his poetry is strongly influenced by folk & country music. He also wrote the novels “Freightliner” & “The Angel From Montgomery”. Currently lives in Nueva Santa María, Mexico City.

Eşref Ozan BAYGIN - Hi! Hayy

Everything, good or bad, gushes out from me.
A hole where I get lost inside myself.
My name wanders in the semahs,
I'm the one crawling underground in pieces.
The road is mine.

If there is no devil, can an angel fit into a dream? (-Who?)
Everything that is not two is a whole and one.
If there is no night, is there any power in the day? (-no)
When minus and plus are hugged, tell me it's one.

If there is no existence, what does non-existence have any meaning? (-No)
If there is no death, can there be eternity? (-No)
If there is, if not, the meaning is interesting.
If the important thing is joy, I found myself.

Everything that happens flows to me like a river.
I stay in the moment and get out of my transparent membrane.
My name wanders around the earth.
I'm the one crawling underground.
The road is mine.

Eşref Ozan BAYGIN
Ozan Baygın (Eşref Ozan Baygın)(Eţref Ozan Baygýn) was born in 1993 in Istanbul. His poems have been published in many magazines and anthologies worldwide. Voice actor (Ne Nerede?) In total he has published six books. In addition to this literary work, he has released seven music albums.

B. Elizabeth Beck - Almost four p.m.

On my treehouse balcony, drunk
on oxygen and Bloody Marys
after hours manicuring gardens.
Sweep, prune, weed, clean out
garage, tossing into garbage
what no longer serves, child gone.

Listening to jazz, pups lie
at feet, wind sweeps through
branches of sugar maple
while goose circles, lonely
without his mate as my brother
meets my mother to plant
flowers too early, but I
remain silent still, playing
the long game as Grateful Dead
cues up Friend of the Devil,

no coincidence, reconciliation
of light and dark, I withdraw
within contentment. Don't
all animals crave comfort?

Yet still/always/never naïve
enough/betrayed too often,
jaded, hurt, still seeking
joy within notes filling spaces
between breezes and bird calls.
Sapphire ring cased in gold
on finger that binds my heart
beyond love I seek on the pond

beyond this balcony moment.
I forgot this. Think time slides
by so quickly until I'm reminded
of new cycle yet again. It's the winds.

Why my heart soars after such
destruction, I don't know. Masochism.

No, wait. Natural self-destruction
delights, charms even as I'm shocked
and dismayed by upheaval yet rejoice,
craving to carve a poem on the page
as Fluffhead cues up, dog of same
name wanders out. Branches
of sugar maple lady mock, enticing
anticipation, only completely,
not quite. Bare branches, last
to open, first to fall. Price

to pay for such majesty. I,
self-proclaimed worshipper
of trees, impatiently patient
wait for her to answer
vernal equinox call to life,
as I focus on face of sapphire
reflecting branches in mini-
composition of everything
contained in one space between
notes that soar as I trust

the pace of life as breath

as much as I trust next note
soaring my soul beyond. Not
whispering winds, but Aries
energy fuels gusts, making
chimes ring, so many strands
I bead, place, set, string
from branches to sing
in accordance to the gold

I weave around wrists.
Look up, spot kids on
neon green kayaks paddling
surface, diamond dappled
like Cave Run Saturdays
I grieve when boat towed.

Yet another mark/clearing/
shift of season I crave
privacy to accept/embrace.
No call to lose time
layering beats on drum today.
Too busy gulping moments,
evoking yoga breath
that launched/catapulted
energy into present. Yet another

brick in time, stacking against
what plagued memories Friday,
April cool melancholy
overcoming senses I accept
quietly, grateful to shroud
silence, isolation in response.
Recourse not reactionary.

B. Elizabeth Beck is a poet who writes fiction. Dancing on the Page (Rabbit House Press, 2024) is her fifth poetry collection. Accents Publishing will publish Swan Songs, her debut collection of short stories. She is the author of the Summer Tour Trilogy. Elizabeth founded two poetry series, Teen Howl, and Poetry at the/ˈtā-bəl/ in Lexington, Kentucky. For more information about Elizabeth: www.elizbeck.com

Robert Bessel - Delivery

The air was thick that day.
95 degrees, maybe 100.
It had rained an hour before.
Hard.
Still the mailman refused to hurry.
His hat and slicker dripped.
His sneakers oozed where he stepped.
But that wasn't enough
to stop him from carrying junk mail
to every address.
And I,
inside and dry,
couldn't help him.
He confessed when I tried:
"Interference is not allowed."
The next day he returned like the day before
Sisyphus with a bag of worthless messages
climbing a mountain of steps
slipping through doors
stuffing the paper into boxes
all to be thrown away.
Some would accuse him
of bringing evil to their door
Some would, if they could,
toss him back to the bottom of his mountain
where he would collect the messages again,
sort them again
and climb again and again.

Robert Bessel lives in the Collinsville section of Canton, Connecticut where he recently served as First Selectman (aka mayor). Since he traded his gavel for a pen, he writes every day and couldn't be happier.

Ellie Bird - Wildflower

In the neon glow of subway tunnels, I shed my old skin like a snake, sloughing off the expectations that clung to me like cobwebs.
I traded my pencil skirt for combat boots, my pearls for a leather jacket, and stepped into the city streets with the swagger of a jazz riff.
The coffee shops became my temples, the baristas my prophets, and I sipped on existential lattes while the world spun madly around me.
I danced with shadows in Greenwich Village, my hips swaying to the syncopated beat of street musicians and subway trains, their rhythms echoing my own transformation.
The moon whispered secrets to me as I wandered through Alphabet City, its graffiti-covered walls telling stories of rebellion, love, and lost dreams.
I painted my lips with defiance, my eyeliner sharp as a switchblade, and claimed my space in this concrete jungle, a wildflower pushing through the cracks.
In the mirror, I saw the reflection of a thousand women who came before me, their struggles etched into my bones, their courage fueling my rebellion.
And so I became woman, not in the quiet corners of a suburban kitchen, but under the neon lights of New York City, where the streets hummed with possibility, and the dead poets whispered, “Write your own damn story.”

Ellie Bird is a Puerto Rican poet from New York City. You can connect with her on Instagram: @words.by.ellie

Bengt O Björklund - there's a moon on the run

from bright war and indiscretion
nights of dubious intent
rule in favor of the stray one

vascular dreams will vessel flow
only because they are fluid
there's an inherit attraction
that can turn any sea into a dream

find me a carpet to fly
in days of raw solicitation
find me a stigma to nourish
when days turn oblique

during the performative years
the coroner made a bold stand
defending the flat ones
and the very thin

rushed to hospital through traffic
the old man could hear the dead
speak of deeds and plain time
laughing in the early morning

Bengt O Björklund born in 1949 is a Poet, painter and percussionist. Bengt started writing poetry in English during his stay in jails in Istanbul in the late sixties. See: I missed Woodstock (Human Error Publishing)
Since then he has published 12 collections, six in Swedish and six in Swedish.

The band Beat Poet Society puts music to his poetry. They're on all musical platforms.
Bengt O Björklund- https://artandmore.store/

Chris Bodor - Irrelevant

It's irrelevant!
It does not apply.
It's irrelevant!
Can, or can't, join me in this chant:
"It's irrelevant. It's irrelevant. It's irrelevant."

It's an elephant.
Let's address the elephant in the room:
"Hello Elephant", wrinkled and gray
"Hello Elephant", you had your day
White elephant sale, pull up the anchor and set sail,
one day I shot an elephant in my pajamas,
so I put down the gun, and stopped wearing pajamas,
now I sleep in the nude. Food for thought. Food of the gods.

This is unacceptable!
I raise my voice another decibel.
Hounded by the birds of prey, when all I want to do is pray.
Being so guarded with my words. I feel discarded.

It's irrelevant! It's an elephant,
and it is departing soon. It is leaving the room.
Say goodbye to the donkey, too.
Let's address the donkey in the room.

Chris Bodor is a first generation American. He was born in Connecticut to an English mother and a Hungarian father. He is currently serving a two-year term as the Florida State Beat Poem Laureate (2023-2025) and he is the Coordinator of the St. Augustine PoetFest. Bodor is the Editor-In-Chief of the international literary journal A.C. PAPA, which stands for Ancient City Poets, Authors, Photographers, and Artists.

Julie Bolt - Sod

Fresh earth, pulling flesh,
Plucking birds, the cleave
Pots simmering the truffles
The wheat, the potato, the leek

We are your echoes
Your heartbeats
Your dry desolate planes
Driven by hunger, by thirst

The thought that hardens
The hand that sculpts
The neck that bends to be stroked
The eyes that close for redemption

We are made of your sacrifice, devotion and tending
We are made of your cheating, killing and lying
Fulfilling your strides, we are mayhem and madness
We are your mountains of moaning

Each generation half-blind
Pulling and pushing
Each will choose whether to survive
To give enough stubborn love, enough radical love

With enough sankalpa breaths
As energy courses through us,
into an unforeseen future, into the sod,
the impossible void

Julie Bolt is an associate professor of English at Bronx Community College/CUNY, currently living in Fort Lee, NJ. Publications include her collection Time Sensitive and her book Border Pedagogy for Democratic Practice. She is in many anthologies. She was a 2023 Best of Net nominee.

R. Bremner - Brazen dreaming

I hear the sounds of brazen dreaming, the gods have sent harpies to wake and break our eardrums! Angry Birds caw, creeping cats screech, doleful dogs wail, ugly oaf ogres trumpet, and there's nary a strumpet to kiss and soothe our aching cochleae, yikes almighty, there's bugs in the sugar, police on the corner, mortgage on the car! And those damnable prose-like earwigs burrowing past the sense and solitude in our minds! When what we need is poetry! I hear America singing but in 2024 it's not Walt's song, it's the stinging dissonance of Realpolitik drowning out the whispers of wisdom, and if we don't wake up soon from this brazen dream we're in for a somnambulism of cackles and squawks and blood oozing and snot dripping and vomit dribbling in a disgraceful mockery of this, the greatest society the world has seen!

R. Bremner has been writing of incense, peppermints, and the color of time since the 1970s, in such venues as International Poetry Review, Paterson Literary Review, Anthem: a Leonard Cohen Tribute Anthology, Climate of Opinion: Sigmund Freud in Poetry,18 jazz poems in Jerry Jazz Musician, and two books and six chapbooks. Ron is a forty-year computer programmer for Pan American World Airways, Continental Airlines, Amtrak, and Citibank. He is a four-time honoree in the Allen Ginsberg Awards.

John Burroughs - Potential Energy

The universe will end in ice
or so a sage I know has - said
but Frost seemed unconvinced
Baldwin spoke of fire next time
and I do not believe in endings
even when we die and decompose
our molecules don't dissipate, still
matter, are uncreated, undestroyed
even at absolute zero, when motion
ceases and all disorder disappears
and your atoms, love, are inducement
enough to give rise to another Big Bang

John Burroughs of Cleveland, OH served as the 2022-2023 U.S. National Beat Poet Laureate, 2019-2021 Ohio Beat Poet Laureate, and founding editor of Crisis Chronicles Press. He is the author of The Wrest of the Worthwhile [2023, Far Queue Press], Rattle & Numb [2019, Venetian Spider Press] and numerous poetry chapbooks. Find him at https://linktr.ee/johnburroughs.

Douglas G. Cala - Blood Pact

Spelunking in sand dunes of lived epiphany, Mercurial moments featuring contemplation risk a cave-in of the mind, Psyche grappling with monoliths of loss, Longwinded, internal monologues threaten to sabotage progression,

Thoughts on the defensive, playing inside the paint, lay ups shattering glass We are either heroes or villains of our own stories, without contractual obligation for repeat appearances Crafting ongoing narratives spanning multiple issues, Flip pages of

graphic novels that encapsulate visual and auditory stimuli, Origin stories and arcs of triumph, sacrifice, victory laps

Craft bigger pictures, see macrocosmic elements take effective root, Honking, hollering, passersby complete passages of a soul's nomadic journey, Selfishness sold in bulk, selflessness cashed out, cards folded, chips in, poker faces drop their mystery Misery loving company, let succulent richness of moments lived provide solace,

No room for morbid solemnity, ancestral flickers act as homages to yesteryear, A healthy dose of self-imposed isolation, limitations leave scars like misplaced tattoos tagged on porous skin, Motor's running, automobile needs a catalyst to reach maximum torque, a home on the road,

traveling tunefully town to town

Techniques can be transitory like transient, globetrotting beings remaking worlds in their likeness Favorability ratings of bleeding-heart politicians' plummet without humanity's recourse

Irrespective of agenda, not everyone is

an accomplice, adjusting your expectations accordingly Don't go catatonic, body seizing up from sensory overload, foaming at the mouth Books filled with portraits of bodies without faces,

no unique identifiers, a bunch of John and Jane Does'

Search for incriminating evidence, crimes against populaces committed by conniving oligarchs who twist power structures for personal gain Make it rain, overflow of capitol yet cities go underfunded,

A pact is made but it isn't signed in blood

Douglas G. Cala is a spoken word performance poet, IT specialist, and photographer/videographer from New York City. His work is widely published in magazines and anthologies. When not writing and performing, Douglas works full time for the Division of Instructional and Information Technology within the NYC Department of Education.

Patricia Carragon - What Was I Made For?
(inspired by Billie Eilish)

My imagination used to float
over the empty courtyard,
away from home and school tensions.
But reality crushed childish fantasies—
my fairy godmothers never paid visits,
my prayers only heard by statues and crosses.

A slap here, a slap there,
a fault here, a fault there.
Never special enough for praise—
constructive criticism would box my ears.
A child's anguish never to be seen or heard,
and school wasn't much better.

Don't cry! You'd only make things worse.
Complaints would only make you ugly.
But in the mirror, I was already there.

I had no purpose but to live.
Sadness grew over the passing years,
stalked me when least expected—
this shadow grew without light,
this shadow was the sandman who stayed
and wouldn't let go of my thoughts.

School had its hierarchy,
but I was a slow learner—
the perennial outsider
who drifted from grade to grade.
Unprepared,
I graduated into adult shoes,
became a cliché,
"rose through the ranks" in the "nine to five world."
My anxiety wore business attire,
my self-worth plucked like feathers.
I had no purpose but to accept this bad script
of which I couldn't edit.

Sadness grew over the passing years,
stalked me when least expected—
this shadow grew without light,
this shadow was the sandman who stayed
and wouldn't let go of my thoughts and body.
The sandman became my lover.
I surrendered to sadness,
and in return,
learned to be happy.

Patricia Carragon's poem, "Wild Is the Wind," (Poets Wear Prada's The Rainbow Project) received a Pushcart nomination. Her debut novel is Angel Fire(Alien Buddha Press). Her books from Poets Wear Prada are Meowku and The Cupcake Chronicles. She hosts Brownstone Poets and is the editor-in-chief of its annual anthology.

Wendy Cartwright - Bad Acting

Around these parts they have a way of saying
you're different
To soften the blow, they say eclectic
Old soul, they say, unique
Tip-toeing around the word weird

What happens when you love weird
When you take it as a compliment
What's wrong with different
Why would anyone want to be a carbon copy
Why would I want to be just like you
In the collective us of every damn day

It takes more courage
To live your life and not mine

People think actors are the richest and most rare
Acting, the most prolific occupation
Least paid profession
Working their asses off pretending
Acting happy, fulfilled
Maximum hours for minimum pay

There's wealth in weird
Abundance in odd

Pockets full of stones and a heart pumping ink
Precious commodities more valuable than paper money
Handing out love and kindness
Instead of nickels and dimes

I wish we were all a little more weird
A little more different
Free to be authentic
Happiness is the key to compassion

Weird concept
Wouldn't that be different

Wendy Cartwright is a poet and author who lives in Columbus, Indiana. Her work has appeared in several poetry collections both inside the US and out and she has had work featured on various online publications. She will release a full volume of poetry mid-2024.

Michael Ceraolo - Free Speech Canto XCII

The National Science Foundation
was established by law in 1950,
and the act creating it said
"The Foundation is authorized to award . . .
scholarships and graduate fellowships . . .
such selections shall be made
solely on the basis of ability"
But when push came to shove,
other considerations would allow
Edward Yellin to be shoved out

In early 1958
Yellin refused to answer five questions
from the House Un-American Committee
about his past Communist activity
(he had left the Party
after the Soviets put down
the Hungarian uprising)
In March of 1960
he was tried and convicted
for contempt of Congress,
and given the maximum sentence
of one year in prison

Remaining out of prison
while his conviction was being appealed,
Yellin sat for a competitive exam,
and scored high enough that in March 1961
he was awarded a $3,800 fellowship
from the NSF

It would be only a few months
before those other considerations
reared their ugly head in the persons
of several representatives:
The head of the NSF said on June 15
"unless we can proved fraud or perjury,
we cannot revoke this fellowship"
Six days later they revoked it,

and it stayed revoked
even though Yellin won at the Supreme Court
almost two years later

Science subservient to politics
is nothing new

(Free Speech Cantos are about the abridging of free speech by nearly everyone)

Michael Ceraolo is a 66-year-old retired firefighter and active poet who has had two full-length books published (Euclid Creek, from Deep Cleveland Press; and 500 Cleveland Haiku, from Writing Knights Press) and has two more in the publication pipeline.

Dr. Ashok Chakravarthy - A Contentment

Yes! Times, good and bad
Moments quick and slow,
Move on and ultimately fade,
Yet few hopes of life still glow,
They appear, but do not fade,
Through poetry they glow.

Memories fade into the past
But the surge of fleeting age,
Gallop without any respite,
But life cannot escape the rage,
But musings keep up the fight,
Providing life, a serene stage.

Caught in the cross-fires of life,
Thirsting for real peace of mind;
Shuttling betwixt desires and grief,
An oasis of uncertainty, I find,
But musings openly script the life,
Blessing a contentment, unbound.

Dr. Ashok Chakravarthy is an established poet whose poems are published in over hundred countries and he's conferred with several national and international awards, doctorates, commendations, titles etc. His poems have been translated to over 40 languages as of now. His poetry arouses Global Peace with the concept of non-violence, supports Anti-Nuclear Manifesto, protecting Environment, protecting Children Rights etc. TEN Poetry Books have been Published so far.

Claire Conroy - September's Son
A Ode for Leonard Cohen

Velvet voice snuggled up to your ear…
Doesn't that song just bring you back?
A port wine heavy on your tongue.
A touch where it needed to be felt.
He'll woo you, September's son can do that to you.
Trapped within a vase, gold in the crack
Finding value and beauty in the broken.
A river to cry, an icy memory of something more
From the edge of frozen Montreal.
Oh LA, barefoot, second hand suit, typewriter,
A shy troubadour hiding in Chateau Marmont.
Smiling, waiting for a miracle to repent against
And afterwards wondered what it meant.
A minstrel made from written word delusion
Of selfless secular meandering Hallelujah.
Summoning Suzanne, in rags and feathers
River maiden of the Salvation Army.
Her beauty shadows his masterpiece.
He is September's son, in fading summer sadness
Leonard crooned and cried, denying Cupid.
Alone, with words, alive with words, alone.
Intense failures waltz through the triumphs
But always reaching, grasping for more than connection.
Alone, the wine kept writing.
Alone, the word kept filling his cup.
Alone.
When Leonard was nine his father died
The boy said goodbye in a note.
With a razor, slit father's tie up the back
Tucked the note into the folds
Rolled it up and planted it in the garden.
What poetry it grew, and spread.
The month of September gave this man.
The loss of a boy gave a poet.
Write the bottle, pour out the page.
Drink the ink and drain the pen.

Claire Conroy has a deep affection for words and their effects on readers. She has self published two books of poems ("Listen" 2018 and "Silent" 2022), a chapbook and has also been published in over a dozen global anthologies. Born in Portsmouth, NH, she is a proud board member of the Portsmouth Poet Laureate Program and lives in Sanford, Maine.

Lesley Constable - (high) Desert Lake

Renew the you, to the interior, the lake still no need to
show to shine the inside of you outward, renew the you, the
still lake of nothing no movement it lays calm unmoving

no need to show or tell what it the dull glow is radiating
quietly by itself and for no one, no one else talking its
language not yours and to no one, the quiet language of
existence, tuned to the ears of stars, the deep slow
sonorous turns of movements sighs deep
in earth connected to your inner ear before trailing up into
the firmament to touch briefly with star to star on its way

it will return to you this voice to shout or to whisper it
doesn't matter it's the same voice
same music sung below the high tones pitched different
and you turn your head tilt your head, a happy dog
knowing you can hear the pitch from a range high up, to
the north, the mountains (of New Mexico) signal you back
home and you will arrive, you will arrive the dirt is nothing
only the sound which emanates from it

I will ask for nothing but the procession of souls, upon
being there, the parasols delicately balance thought,
the depth of love for you colors of each in harmony with
moon the salt air rising above sound, its mist rising, risen
high like sun

I ride your horse, Manuel, in the wake of you,
in the wake of the gone one and we travel together
knowing loss mourning
and like the sound of dirt we both know we are eternal

Lesley Constable - poet, painter, modern dancer, gonzo visionary since birth, dual UK/US citizen + lives in MX, 60s rock 'n' roll Hippie chick, road-tripper, vintner (dandelion wine), architect/builder of 4 houses (including straw bale), arts journalist/art critic, art gallery curator, University studio arts instructor, US High School English/Poetry teacher - dips her toe, then whole body/heart/soul into it, the all, and stays there.

Jason Conway - Who says there's no place for Mustangs in poetry open mics?

Let me set the scene...

An intimate poetry gig in a local paddock
A herd of poets sign up for a slot
take a seat and chomp on their numbers
as an expectant audience awaits

A bareback rider grips the mic
Their lips release a feral horse
as hippophiles fix on white-hot words that flash
a thunderstorm and necks prickle
followed by a round of claps

Apart from a single neigh at the back of the room
from a startled punter who thinks poetry
isn't poetry with expletives
a different language out of context
That all poems should have horseshoes
with rules nailed into them

I bet they wish they could crack a whip
force the diction of Mustangs
They believe poems should be domesticated
given rosettes for dressage

I like jockeys that flex every linguistic muscle without blinkers
and their emphasis delivered raw
I share their passion for urgency
The visceral beauty of their honesty

To those in the stable that say
Poetry needs a saddle
and wild words left in pasture
I say

Mierda de caballo.

Jason Conway is a professional daydreamer, director of the Gloucestershire Poetry Society and editor of Steel Jackdaw magazine. His poetry is published in Poetry Bus, The Poetry Village, Impspired, Wildfire Words, Dreich, Fevers of the Mind, Ink Sweat and Tears, and on BBC Upload. He has an MA in Creative Writing from Bath Spa University, and is an Arts Council funded poet.

Mikayla Cyr - Post-Immersion Syndrome

Running in circles
Running out of breath
Scars lay white and weathered
upon skin like train tracks
A wrecked car of adolescence
A memorial of youth
and unbridled feeling
Simmering rage sinks into the liver
Where we taught it to live
Where we tried to drown it
Fix the car and polish the knife
They tell you
They don't mention the demons
have Olympic gold medals in
swimming
High dives and butterflies
Their trophies gave us metal poisoning
The ribbons stuck in our throats
Laughter in the face of
healthy coping mechanisms
Synchronized cynicism makes
bigger waves than the ethanol
ever dreamed it could
Every burning sip gave them
more to practice with
Every breath, but a joke
no one's told yet
Did you become another vessel
for the darkness to win?
I, myself
couldn't afford another crash

Mikayla Cyr is a Portland, ME native with an affinity for nature and the arts, as well as a passion for poetry that's lived for decades.

Binod Dawadi - They Think I Am Nothing

They think I can't earn
I can't look for a family
I can't do government jobs
I can't go foreign to earn
All my friends and relatives
They are changing their life
By earning
Why I can't I don't know

I also tried hard to earn
As well as become rich from poor
But I can't
Maybe I haven't got
A good destiny
Or luck like them
But I should work hard
I should fulfill my aims
As well as my dreams
I should not lose my hope

Binod Dawadi, the author of The Power of Words, is a master's degree holder in Major English. He has worked on more than 1000 anthologies published in various renowned magazines. His vision is to change society through knowledge. So he wants to provide enlightenment to the people through his writing skills.

Chris Dean - the women

Footnotes and Mrs.,
relegated to supporting
cast and crew
existing in the
shadows of greatness.
That's how I've read
The Women described.

I found your words
later in life,
past the times of passings,
but they still sing.
They cry.
They scream off the page,
laden with rage, anguish
and hope.
They speak across
years and graves,
in dreams and daydreams.

Their force burned a path
for those of us
who heard the call
and their power
cast the circle
in which we now stand,
in Sacred Space
their passion created.

And when we speak
with our voice,
with your voice,
with the voice
of an entire world,
our words bear
the autographs and echoes
of each and every one
of your names.

Chris Dean writes from the heart of Indiana. Their work has been featured by Cajun Mutt Press, Fevers of the Mind, Dumpster Fire Press as well as Gal's Guide To The Galaxy's "Nourish" and "Ovation" from Jimmy Broccoli. Their debut Book of poetry, Tales From a Broken Girl, was released in 2023 by Storeylines Press.

Arlene DeMaris - Dream Kitchen

My mother makes contact, blows the smoke
of her ghost into the new cabinets, unmolds
grits from a coffee can, slices and fries in bacon grease

over the blue jewels of gas jets that light the six-burner
stove. No punch holes in the wall. No need to hide
the sharps. All the appliances fresh out of their boxes

here in the kitchen she could not, her father the peanut farmer
could not, the girls at the plant could not imagine, slipping
their names and addresses into crates of nickel bags

for pen pals who would not marry. Or would: the grocery clerk
who unpacked her, opened wounds on worn floorboards, tied
her apron tight. If I could crawl back through her, shrink

to a red dot of flesh then nothing, she still would not live
long enough. **Will I ever live to see it**, she asks, shade at my table
watching the astonishment of a flat screen on the wall

tuned to reruns of I Love Lucy, chocolates falling off
conveyor belts, the laugh track soothing as ocean waves.

Arlene DeMaris is a freelance writer and editor living in Avon, Connecticut.

Vivian Demuth - Buddha Bar

At the Buddha Bar just around the corner from Starbucks, some people drink in the shadows while others stand looking toward the lights as if to be beamed up. Some stand on their heads because their tired of sitting, but no one minds at the Buddha Bar where buddhas and dakinis chuckle at the big screen featuring endless G.I. Joe wars. I like to sip on a kindly wine and watch monks and nuns recite the Fire Sermon from a tightrope strung above. They stir fear while I ride the burning neurons of my mind, until I quietly burp--Ah, nothing but air--and wait for the next poem, and freedom from suffering for all.

Vivian Demuth is the author of the eco-poetry book, Fire Watcher (Guernica Editions) and the ecological novels, Bear War-den, (Inanna Publications) and Eyes of the Forest (Smoky Peace Press). Her poetry and fiction have been published in journals and anthologies in the United States, Canada, Mexico, and Europe and have been broadcast on public radio. She has worked as a fire lookout observer in the Rocky Mountains and with un-housed people in New York city. www.viviandemuth.com

Lee Desrosiers - Take Five

Back when I was flying solo
a date took me to hear Dave Brubeck
and his quartet, around 1995.

I remember watching the bass player
because strings always pull me in –
his expression changed with every note.

Jazz is taking a song and changing it –
a departure, like in a poem when
you were writing about a date

then suddenly you are on top of the hill
looking down on the concert below
and you grow wings and fly.

Lee Desrosiers (they/them) is a native New Yorker who moved north to hear the crickets and has lived in western Massachusetts and New England for the last 30+ years. They are currently working on two books simultaneously. Lee's latest book of poetry is Keeping Planes in the Air (Salmon Poetry 2020).

William F. DeVault - Passover in Palestine

the bitter herbs of a Passover in Palestine.
American complicity in genocide
for political expediency.
can't show weakness to the hungry cowards
begging for approval from the cruel bullies
with human sacrifice to prove your fealty
in this reality game show
that slaughters and burns
children and women in vile provocation
for the next generation of terrorists
who will live for their revenge
against those who burned their babies
from alive unto death.
with no moral or scriptural validity.
Pesach of slaughtered lambs
on both sides of cycles of hate.
bitter herbs, indeed
the unleavened flesh of innocents
consumed with a theological zeal
and never beating swords into plowshares.

William F. DeVault was the US National Beat Poet Laureate from 2017 through 2018. He has toured throughout the US, giving readings from coat to coast. He currently serves as the CEO of Venetian Spider Press, as well as continuing to write in manic bursts. His religion is poetry. He has been married and divorced twice and fathered 3 magnificent children.

John Dorsey - When The Eclipse Was Every Day
for damian rucci

i can't expect you to know
what it felt like to play kickball
under the moonlit Pennsylvania sky in 1986
when the magic of the wind
was just something we felt in our bones
when we called our god Houdini
when we found love in shopping malls
& video arcades that had sprung up like temples
under the sky's infinite grace
when we waited for Halley's comet
listening with our ears to the ground
as if cupping seashells on dry land
i can't expect you to know all that
that the moon was once a hopeful thing
& that now i shake at night
instead up sleeping soundly
because sleep is for the young
& those unemployed by constant worry
now i pace back & forth
sweeping up moon dust
in nonexistent dreams
& have nowhere to put it all
but i'll tell you
when you run out of hope
you'll look up at the sky with wonder
& see a boy in your reflection
& you will miss it.

John Dorsey is the former Poet Laureate of Belle, MO. He is the author of several collections of poetry, including Which Way to the River: Selected Poems: 2016-2020 (OAC Books, 2020), Sundown at the Redneck Carnival, (Spartan Press, 2022, and Pocatello Wildflower, (Crisis Chronicles Press, 2023). He may be reached at archerevans@yahoo.com.

Michael E. Duckwall - Against the Tides:

Look for people swimming against the tides
the ones who swim out in the undertow, to save another.

The ones who risk it all, to lift up family and friends.
The ones who will help out a stranger, when they have
nothing to gain.

People who live for change, thriving in the dark cold light
of a full moon. The nights crazy runs wild and the currents
pull at our souls.

When we swim into the undertow and risk it all
to save anyone reaching out their hand, when they're
drowning.

Look for people who see a need and fill it, asking for nothing
but acceptance. Just to be accepted, for living their life.

Look for these people, look in the mirror and hope to see
one looking back.
These are my people, those who swim against the tides.

I can only hope to see one in the mirror, living a life that pulls
me under every chance it gets. Making me remember,
making me forget the best

the worst and as I'm sinking towards the ocean floor
I think of love and in this moment, I reach out my hand

I'm going under, hoping someone sees me, people who are
swimming
against the tides, into the undertow, my people. More often
than not

I sink into the dark, I'm reaching out
I love you.

Michael E. Duckwall was born and raised in the Ohio valley. He has a couple of chapbooks you can find online and also co-authored a limited edition handmade chapbook with Chad M. Horn. Michael was a featured poet at the last Gonzofest in Louisville Ky. His poetry, artwork and photography are in numerous magazines and online features.

Carlos Raúl Dufflar 12/1/2017 - In the Passing Years

In the passing years, the eagle flies above
Glazing at the sky
For I believe in the written word
With kindness to Pachamama – Mother Earth
Sharing our verses throughout Turtle Island
Love, smile, and laughter
Before the moon rises
When the rainbow conscious dance
Of the very song of love over sickness
We value the Earth
In which water gives us life
Yes, I remember Jimi Hendrix performing
At the Café Wha
In the 1960s
"All Along the Watchtower"
In the harshness of the years of the war
It's really sad that they spend
Hundreds of billions of dollars a year
And not on kindness of the War on Poverty
As The Buffalo Springfield on the radio
Singing "For What It's Worth"
There are thousands of people on the street
And something in the air
Two wrongs don't make a right
Spring Mobilization Against the War in Vietnam
People were gathering in Central Park
Marching in front of the United Nations
As Dr. Martin Luther King, Jr. speaks to the crowd
Let's have peace on Earth
With 500,000 people cheering and chanting
Bridging a new light
Verses that flow of your imagination
As you enter inside of the Community Church
And sit and listen on the third month
A laughter and a joyfulness
Eyes open towards the Sun
As the sound of bebop is blown
As Sun Ra's Arkestra enters from the front door
People are jumping up and gathering in a circle

Dancing to the melody of traveling the spaceways
From somewhere in between towards the Mothership
Travel the spaceways

Carlos Raúl Dufflar As a New Generation Beat Poet Laureate (2023-Lifetime), Carlos Raúl Dufflar has been traveling on the road from the Northeast and performing at museums, cafés, rallies, along the Peace Way, and working on a new book.

Mercedes Dugger - The Dead Flowers

The dead flowers remain in place
Though they are long gone from her vase
Indifferent to summer breeze
Impervious to winter freeze
Dead flowers always haunt this space.
A new bouquet cannot erase
The sadness on the woman's face
Everywhere she looks she sees
The dead flowers.
Wishing those flowers had the grace
To disappear without a trace
Away from her contentment flees
Dead flowers fill her with unease
She knows that she cannot replace
The dead flowers.

Mercedes Dugger is a California native and lifelong resident of the San Francisco Bay Area. As a parochial school student during her formative years, Mercedes excelled in academic subjects and art. Her love of literature and art persisted throughout her childhood and adolescence. Mercedes was married for nearly three decades, until the untimely death of her husband in 2013. She spent another decade living the quiet life of a widow. In 2023, Mercedes ventured out to see if she could find love again. She did, in the person of the poet with whom she wrote Morning Tanka.

Kapardeli Eftichia - At flapping wings

Three angels with excess
peacefulness
on one virgin dome
a simplistic church
hanging

Flowers measure
forces
on stone slits

The people grow
in loneliness
hungry for love

The deserted streets
Hold the calcined
sun of summer
birds waiting

In the long journey
promise roots stretching
at flapping wings
in the cities of the world
colors awaken to light

ΣΤΟ ΧΤΥΠΗΜΑ ΤΩΝ ΦΤΕΡΩΝ

Τρεις άγγελοι με περίσσεια
γαλήνη
σε έναν παρθένο τρούλο
μιας απλοϊκής εκκλησιάς
κρέμονται

Λούλουδα μετρούν την
δύναμη τους
στις σχισμές της πέτρας

Οι άνθρωποι μεγαλώνουν
στην μοναξιά
διψούν για αγάπη

Οι δρόμοι έρημοι
κρατούν τον πυρωμένο
Ήλιο του καλοκαιριού
τα πουλιά περιμένουν

Στο μακρινό ταξίδι
η υπόσχεση ρίζες απλώνει
στο χτύπημα των φτερών
στις πόλεις του κόσμου
ξυπνούν τα χρώματα στο φως

Kapardeli Eftichia from Greece, has a degree in art conservator and a Doctorate from Arts And Culture World Academy. International Ambassador of the International Chamber of Writers and Artists LLC, Member of the World Poets Society and World Academy of Art and Culture | Facebook poetas del mundo, member of the IWA, member of Ε.Ε.Λ.Σ.Π.Η The Union of Greek Writers-Authors of the Five Continents , member of the INTERNATIONAL SOCIETY OF GREEK LITERATURES-ARTISTS-DEEL and PEL (the world association of writers in Greece) Panhellenic Union of Writers http://eftichiakapa.blogspot.gr/2013_10_01_archive.html

Les Epstein - Once Upon a Time: The Second Avenue Deli

This soup has balls.
Matzah Balls that is
Where in its depths
The celery's fine
And the onion not so intrusive
The kosher bird's shredded
So finely it could hang about my teeth
As a fiber installation
And never lose flavor.

The withered noodles float sassy parve
(I have an elbow in my ribs.)
No salt, please, this broth need be spare.
(I've dropped my damn spoon.)
Curse me if I should have a good time.
(Three peppercorns should clear tightening nasals.)
I should wear its bay leaf in my hair.
(Matzah still has that blocking effect.)

On the sidewalk
Outside a steamed window
Ice covers metallic plates
with names swathed within a Mogen David:
Kamińska, Goldfaden
a Jacobs, a Schwartz, an Adler or two…
Formerly spectacular on boards since crushed still
Think Adler's Yiddishkeit Lear or
Thomashefsky's Parsifal sung in the same tongue…

Shining Folksbiene stars
Until snow buries their melodious monikers,
Much like the mashed ball
Covers the delicious distance
Within my bowl.
Swimming events within this soup would sell tickets
Though in waiting too long
It would become far too cold for a dip.

Les Epstein is a poet, playwright and opera librettist. His books include Sleep Cinematic: A Golem's Quartet (Gnashing Teeth), Kip Divided (Finishing Line), Lorenzo by the Ghost Light (Gnashing Teeth).and Teddy Orloff and the Three Onions(Gnashing Teeth). Recent journal credits include Reedy Branch Review, Otherwise Engaged, and Clinch Mountain Review, as well as the anthologies Pain & Renewal (Vita Brevis Press) and Ohio Bards Poetry Anthology (Local Gems Press). He teaches in Roanoke, VA.

Sandra Feen - Sooner or later

you wake up to nibbles in a diagonal row on your neck.
Someone waited until you wriggled under your blanket,
zipped your eyes shut. After they bit, they gaze lower:
toes wait as petit four.

Once you saved cobalt blue beer bottles
because your mother liked deep azure glass,
and you allowed an empty one to sit in the garage for a spell.
One Saturday, you're dancing around your kitchen,
feel like sprucing everything up, bring one in,
scrub off the grolsch advertisement in a kitchen sink
of hot water and dish washing liquid. You squirt a little
soap into the bottle's neck, combine lukewarm water,
smell stench you think is sticky beer residue, shake shakeit to
Loverboy's *Everybody's Working for the Weekend,*

then when you turn the bottle upside down, let soap suds
splash onto your upright hand, including a black mouse
that plops into your palm like a wooden block,
stiff legs saluting your tune. Your scream doesn't deter
your cat, who crouches by the corner of the fridge,
sniffing someone there on its other side,

and on the deck floor,
last night's evidence: a drizzle of tomato seeds
where a possum stopped by.
He ate your best from your garden,
then made a mark on your deck door
where he wanted to nose in.
A centipede's been waiting behind

that stack of books underneath your desk,
where eight months
of swearing you'd get organized
did not exorcise their residence,
or his. Sooner or later you will face it:
you pay for a home you never really own,
just as your body is on borrowed time too.

You missed noticing yesterday's new hole
a groundhog dug under your foundation.
The possum will sneak through that entrance soon.
One morning you'll wake with gnawed armpits. You were
wearing that eucalyptus deodorant that became a snack:
your demise,now your eyes, black olives, and nose, pink
and long in violated fury.

Sandra Feen is the 2022-2024 Ohio Beat Poet Laureate and author of three poetry collections. She has co-written her forthcoming collection, There Is A Rock On Martin Avenue with Cliff Treyens, which will be published by Venetian Spider Press. She co-hosts The Muse's Mic, with James Bryant.

Mary Eichhorn Fletcher - Rachel, sister of Leah*

"Now Laban had two daughters. The name of the older was Leah, and the name of the younger, Rachel." Genesis 29:16

People forget (sometimes)
(most of the time)
that I am her sister
and she is mine
and that she loved me first
before he loved me or before
I learned to love him.
(Although for that
it did not take me long.)

She had her strengths and weaknesses
(like me).
I loved her long black hair;
she loved my blue and shiny eyes.
We had foibles and quirks,
longings and sadnesses and dreams --
like all of us.
Sisters fight, of course,
and do not agree
and are petty and jealous
and sometimes keep score
(and so did we).
But it was our father
(for whatever his true reasons were)
who authored the deception
which caused much of the trouble later.

Leah had ten sons.
I had two
(after too many years of trying).
I did not live to see them grow up
or know if they loved each other
after I died.
I hope my sister raised them
as her own --
and came to love them as I did.

(Some day Leah will tell me.)

I hope the boys loved each other
the way that Leah and I loved each other,
at least when we were young.
Some day she will tell me that too.

* The account of Rachel and husband Jacob and her sister Leah and their families is told primarily in Chapters 29-31 in the book of Genesis in the Bible. Rachel is referred to elsewhere in both the Old and New Testaments.

Mary Eichhorn Fletcher lives in an old mill town in Connecticut with her husband (and the occasional cat who wanders through and decides to stay). She has been writing poetry for more than 70 years and may be reached by email at AtticMary@gmail.com.

Bryan Franco - A Treatise On The Edibility Of Onion Skins

I don't recognize who
I see in the mirror.

It's not the unkempt beard or
the baggage under my eyes.

It's the onion trapped inside my soul
unable to peel away its inedible outer layers
because my heart has been broken so many times,
its skin is made of several haphazardly-wrapped layers of
duct tape: frayed edges
attracting emotional detritus like a lint trap in a dryer:
encased in mistakes and wrong decisions:
furthering inaccessibility
creating an impenetrable barrier
to love and happiness
that can't be breached
via sad love songs
or tear jerkers
or ear nibbles
or slow-moving fingertips.

There is no prince charming
capable of kissing away history.

Munitions experts would be
wasting their time with dynamite.

Superman might go blind
if he tried to melt it with his stare.

I am resigned to accept
my permanently damaged heart
beating and trying to find ways
to find love despite
all the duct tape and detritus
that might only exist
inside my mind.

Bryan Franco is a neurodivergent, gay, Jewish poet from Brunswick, Maine. He is published in the US, Australia, England, Germany, Holland, India, Ireland, and Scotland. He hosts Café Generalissimo and is a painter, sculptor, and culinary genius. His book "Everything I Think Is All in My Mind" was published in 2021.

Dayna Genevieve - Camera shy

In the floodlights of the barn stage
and the footnotes of your baby self torn

the scars that come with a
beautiful body youth

of ruining and reflection

be a believer
be a skeptic

men
trying to con you into being older than you are
in the first sundown

it's grand slam sham

revolutions and catastrophic daydreams
night holds the only survivors

the auroras are all in your head

flashes of brilliant color fleeting
seismic rumblings crumble
pillars

the house is heavy

Indian pajamas
Danish hair
playing backgammon

alone

who's going to come in to protect you
when you hold the only key to the house
and the door is always open

the decades you'll have to travel

to safety

a madwoman, a crow
breaching dusk
upon us

the cowering hours
of sin within

a breaking down
or breaking in

expect the unacceptable

I miss the days
of me noticing
you noticing me

the spark gaze

that brought me your melodies
to sing and play with in my hands
and hair

beyond the orchid
entangled there

and the wide angle lens

blurring edges retreat
hiding from the blinding bulb

Dayna lives, writes and hosts happenings on her ranch in Northern California.

Mimi German - War Poem #42

(Galilee Fumitory, an extremely rare flower in Israel's Hanita Forest near Lebanon)

did you mean by saying
from the river to the sea
that you yearn to discover
the flowering path

that you have seen
the wild tulips hatch
upon the northern hills
and spotted the rarest flower
like a violet-colored peace
so extremely rare
seen by too few to believe
it could be real

when you saw the flowering lily
felt its petals in your soul
that light and grace grow plentiful
from the hills of galilee
south into the sea
did it show you that of flowers
all are we

i'm certain this must be
what you meant when you said
from the river to the sea
of flowers all are we
of flowers all are we

Mimi German
Oregon Beat Poet Laureate (2023-2025)

Helen Nunley Gilbert - Epitaph

Make my bed with sheets of rain
Blankets of snow
Cloud pillows
Thunderous dreams
Storms
Paint my ceiling with stars.

Helen Nunley Gilbert is an artist, writer, poet, and a lover of David Bowie, reading, horses and cats. She resides in Colorado.

Daniela Gioseffi - Waiting Women: Goddesses of Life

The weighty everlasting wait of waiting women,
waiting for men to return from the hunt for dinner,
from war with smoking guns. Through centuries,
they bow their heads in supplication over soup pots
or grey washtubs and dream of romance rarely fulfilled
after they'd given all to God the Father
-- tall authority commanding from on high;
Yahweh or Zeus, who say, "Wait for a kind word from me!"
And so, they waited, and wait, tied by their love for children,
sons or daughters. They wait to make a home for them
to return to their tables for nurturing.

If they go out after the men, they are deemed aggressive,
untrustworthy,
prying, bad, dirty, unseemly, whorey, unfeminine,
unwomanly, so they waited,
and wait, empty vessels lined up and prepared
for action in the kitchen,
cleaned and ready for whatever is poured into them,
soups and sperm,
to simmer as they nibbled chocolates or bread for love,
or stirred in anger, raging with their spoons.

Ready for the attack, diaphragms in place,
gonads poised, ready for the squirmy dance of travelling sperm,
racing toward waiting ova floating down to meet his spark,
waiting for life to come to them,
waiting for peace to explode in them,
waiting for love to fuse in them, counting on it, alone
with their children, all over the planet, they wait
for the fire bombs of angry erections or the erect bayonets
to come stabbing out of the jungle,
wait for firm life to be sucked
into their bellies where they are reborn
as from a white hole in space,
the opposite of darkness which they make
with their milky breasts, life from flesh into flesh.
On and on into and out of
their legs from which all come and go peeping beneath their

skirts, rising or falling Mother Earth waiting for sun or rain to fall upon her belly, seeds to be planted, with light, death, tears come, and they threaten with weeping cries of guilt,
and so, to awaken from this wait, oh, Goddesses of Life, pacing longing, waiting for moonbeams to shine through the torn veil in the sky, clouded mystery we are even to ourselves as we come from our own insides and men puzzle at us and love/hate us as their mothers, wanting to be held, comforted, wanting to be free, always telling usdouble
messages of love me, let me go and be free and keep me, and so we wait and slowly dry out, naked arms once thin girl's grown plump and tired, bodies soft tipped growing frost over their lips, nerves,as we wait, slowly wrinkling in time, imposed silence.

Fingers feel, curl around our angers,
as we wait, fire's
burning low,
As we wait, saying to ourselves, ah, when I was young
he wanted me so, when I was young he chased me
over the wet grass
and captured and put me in this place of waiting,
for him to come
and fill me with angry death, a vessel among cups, sauce pans,
sink, washtub, bowls, dishes, and vases, waiting
at the windows, widows' walks on rooftops,
faces of waiting women, endlessly,
waiting and searching out to a rocking cradle of sea

Daniela Gioseffi is an American Book Award winning author of 18 books, her most widely read is an anthology first published by Simon & Schuster and reissued by The Feminist Press, Women on War; International Writings from Antiquity to the Present. In print for nearly 30 years! She is a noted feminist since the 1960's.
https://www.poetryfoundation.org/poets/daniela-gioseffi

Jane 'SpokenWord' Grenier - Pain & Pleasure

I am the bonfire from hell
I spit flames from a burnt-out shell
danger danger from 1st degree burns
words in motion at the point of no return
scorched this poet's pen in flames
arguing with mind that play blame games
incinerated syllables ash the truth
my talk has eyes that see through you
this poet's tongue is not for sale
I do not ride the sacrificial trail
sharing pain and pleasure with the inside invader
where shadowed monsters lurk within
burrowing deep beneath my skin
drain my soul
deny my totem pole
waggin' my finger at my capacity for self-destruction
threatening my future's earthly construction
straddling that third rail
drinking arsenic cocktails
I watch the candle drip
through a clear and steady flame
perpetually tortured by the waiting game
charred my soul on the embers of charcoal
waxing my madness
white washing my canvas
denying the never ever
the trickster ever clever
Confusing my control
with a complicated flow
was that the red pill
or purple ozsley's will?
Come out Come out wherever you are.
Contemplating the Darkside's endless journey
waging hunger games with brutal adversity
in a fucking hell where the devil lies laughing
his ravenous fire perpetually crackling
misery charges the air
his ecstasy is my nightmare
caging me in

begging for freedom
fighting for life
holding on tight
to my immortal light

Jane 'SpokenWord' Grenier

"Among the handful of poets - published and/or performing today - one mind that thrills is the one inside Jane Grenier's brain. Communicating directly with the nerve endings of her hands, her poetry shocks and thrills." Raoul daGama. "Like those of the Beats, The Last Poets, Gil Scott-Heron and others Jane is accompanied by Albey Balgochian's, rumbling contrabass - adding double the gut-punch to her words." Jazz daGama. From solos, to bands, she brings her spoken word to a diverse set of venues from museums, festivals, slam lounges, art galleries, clubs, busking street corners and living rooms everywhere.
https://janespokenword.com

Haden - Punk Rock Iguana in Costa Rica

Iguana in our pathway
he says, *Ye shall not pass today*
his muscled arms and puffed chest say
don't you dare try to walk this way
his rough click toenails grip the clay
the place behind him is where we stay
he gives zero frijoles on this sunny day
don't fence me in, I'll make you pay
just you try it, you'll get thrashed, bae

Hayden is Poet Laureate at Sinclair College, award-winning Humanities Professor with a debut collection,American Saunter, forthcoming (FlowerSong Press, 2024), followed by her second, Old World Wings (Wild Ink Publishing, 2025). She received the River Heron's Editors' Choice Prize and lives with her family and rescue babies, including a blind, three-legged pup.

Shafkat Aziz Hajam - The Lost Dream

The lost dream, I dreamt again ,
Couldn't fulfil it, oh ! it caused pain .
Its beauty was not altered a bit ,
Not even my desire for it .
I dreamt it again but untimely .
I could only cry helplessly .
My cry and sigh it could hear,
Though it yearned , it wasn't fair
For it to be the dream of mine again
As like me , him it would cause pain

Shafkat Aziz Hajam is from Kashmir, India.
He is a poet, reviewer and co-author. He is the author of two children poetry books titled as The cuckoo's voice and the canary's voice.

Fin Hall - Amnesia Hotel

Somewhere in the back of my mind
I have travelled there
It is the place we always meant to go
Where memories are best forgotten
You've been there, you know you have
Even though you don't remember
Its closer than you think
Small bar, cheap drink
Concrete everywhere
Nothing to make you want to go back
At least I don t recall it had

The dusty receptionist
Looked a lot like
The dusty bartender
Who had a dusty dog called,
Yup,
Dust
Looked like a crossed between a border collie and a sloth
Moved like the latter
And couldn't be bothered to bark like the former

Its the kind of place,
Well, like the dream you thought you had
And woke up not knowing anything about it
Other that you thought you dreamed
Timeless
In the way of broken clocks
Always reading 17 minutes past 8
Not sure if it is morning
Or evening
But I know is green
Unlike the Amnesia Hotel
Which is beige
In a grey way

The only vegetation is some sorry looking weeds
Growing begrudgingly in the cracks at the bottom of the sign
pole

Even tumbleweeds avoid it
If it has to
Boring cars park in the shadow of shadowy buildings
Shacks, disguised as rooms
The evening sun doesn't hang about long enough
To offer relief

One night stays
Passers by
Going to to places they want to remember
Forgetting why they stopped there
Middle of nowhere.
Its still somehow, somewhere
I guess

She met me by the vending machine
The one outside
At the rear of the laundry room
Where the heat blended with the noise and the condensation from the washers
No dryers
Just a line of old rope where the linen was hung and dried

We chatted about nothing much
As we drank our warm and fizzy,
Low brand colas
Then went our separate ways
As much excitement as you could get
In they place of forget
Somewhere out there.

But don't ask for directions
I couldn't tell you where.

Fin Hall, is a multi published and performance poet, film maker, zoom and live show host, publisher and collaborator from North East of Scotland.

Brian Hassett - Ode to Jack

Jack fights back
from off the beaten track,
still alive
at one hundred
as if any any of us wondered
if that would happen!
after his track star sprint
through the pages of history,
seeing around corners like Neal at the wheel,
knockin over grammar cops
and blowin past the door stops
to hidden darkened jazz joints
puffin on a Mezz joint
never missing the point
of dancing with the mad ones
and singing with the sad ones
and drinking with the bad ones
and skipping past the madhouse
and steering clear the jailhouse
heading for his mom's house
to write another epic
soaring while he's manic
catchin all the magic
of mysteries dark & vast;
he channeled spirits till the last
he hitched the roads, had a blast,
he wrote it down really fast.
Now it's 50 since he passed —
let's hoist his flag up our mast!
salute the work he amassed,
"Have you ever seen a canon so vast?"
So let us all
take a moment to thank —
the Pollard for the books
the Young Prometheans for the camaraderie
the Columbia cabal for "The New Vision"
Neal Cassady for The Letter
Bill Cannastra for The Paper
Joan Haverty for the apartment

Malcolm Cowley for the championing
Gilbert Millstein for the reviewing
David Amram for the playing
Allen Ginsberg for the . . . everything
Lowell for the Celebrating
You for the Being
We for the Seeing
The glowing light of the golden eternity!
Thank you Jack for all you shone.

Brian Hassett is the author of a literary nonfiction Beat Trilogy — The Hitchhiker's Guide to Jack Kerouac (2015), How The Beats Begat The Pranksters & Other Adventure Tales (2017) and On The Road with Cassadys & Furthur Visions (2018). He also contributed to The Rolling Stone Book of The Beats and Kerouac on Record, and created the "Jack on Film" show featuring his every portrayal on the big or small screen. He has performed Kerouac's prose and his own poetry on stage in London, Amsterdam, Toronto, New York, L.A., S.F., New Orleans, Lowell & many other places.

Joan Hawkins - Coltrane Changes

Every my-life era
has its own Jazz Man.
First it was Miles,
with his Cool Jazz
and Hard Bop sounds.
Bitches Brew – Its trippy
album cover, an acid staple
in every hip 1970 living room.

Miles was my main Jazz Man
for years. Decades even. Workin'
and Steamin' through shit jobs and
long commutes; child-rearing and
graduate school. Then came late
marriage, Kind of Blue afternoons—
making love by the fire.
Ghost traces of dark soot
left on my body by Skip's
smoky hands. Sketches of Spain.

Then –well- shit happens.
And when it happened,
big time, to me—
that's when I started
seriously listening to Coltrane.

Now, Trane's a demanding cat.
Even more than Miles.
I listened to Trane's Blues and
Blue Train, over and over-
writing long blog posts. Fashioning
Skip's cancer into something
knowable. Tellable. Comforting
family and friends with
angel-headed hipster stories,
as though we were all young again.

Bad news or good, blue was my color.
And I played Trane's two, too-blue, albums

until I knew every minor fall and major lift
by heart. Then a friend sent a 4 a.m.
You Tube link for “Naima.” Trane
in performance, playing the piece. And,
well, I didn’t exactly break up with Miles.
But I did move him a bit further down the playlist.

It’s complicated. Cuz you see Trane’s a shape-shifting
Jazz Man. Just the cat for non-resolve and e-volving
situations.
Complex chord cycles. Sharp substitutions. Changesso
uniquely his, they still bear his name.
Coltrane Changes, we call them. Coltrane Changes.

Coltrane changes seem to be my road map now.
And who knows where ‘Trane, still my main
Jazz Man, will lead. There’s a St. John Coltrane
Church in San Francisco. African Orthodox,
they style it. I don’t know much about Africa.
But in every my-life era, jazz has been prophetic;
jazz has been divine. And San Francisco is my home town.

So maybe Trane will take me home. Maybe he’ll
lead me to another Jazz Man. Another my-life era.
Or maybe, maybe, he will take me back.
Back to my own Dark God.

Joan Hawkins is the author of Cutting Edge: Art Horror and the Horrific Avant-Garde and, with Alex Wermer-Colan, co-editor of William S. Burroughs Cutting Up the Century. Her creative work includes School and Suicide, The Burroughs Hour, and a spoken word CD (with Kyle Quass) Pragis. She lives in Bloomington, Indiana with her cat, Izzy Isou.

David Henri - If these printed words could speak,

they would be vociferous with voice,
they would stand upright on this page
right here at the coffee shop,
speaking up in unison,
creating a pop-up poetry event,
excuse us for a minute,
may we have your attention please,
let's take a moment to honor the pacifists,
raise a cup to the activated catalysts,
the change makers,
the artists, the musicians, the writers,

if these letters of words could walk,
they'd hold hands
in a line across the street
and march up main,
spelling out *LOVE,*
then {H}{O}{P}{E} emblazed
on brightly colored tees,
each personality signing out
their short word part with optimism,
Equity banner leads a bongo drum line!
then a (Truth) parade float,
Joy dancing as three lovely sprites,
a consonant followed by two vowels,
with locked elbows <J><U><S><T><I><C><E>
marches chins high with determined steps,
[P][E][A][C][E] on protest posters
moving up and down to attract attention,

if these printed words could hear,
they would listen carefully
for clues from the waterfall,
the moans of the suffering
would ring in ears,
sounds of alarms mixed with faint music,
echoes of echoes of echoes
would fade into the canyon,

if these words could animate,
they would be cartoons alive,
  a colorful parade of characters,
antics of acrobats
   and jugglers of small i and j dots,
      readers would be amused,

if these words could read
they would read their faces in the mirror
 and recite themselves word for word

David Henri and his wife Barbara live in New Hartford CT. David developed into a poet later in life, and has self published 4 short books.

He writes about sustainability and mind expansion through contemplation.

Roxanne Hoffman - The Burden Of The Body

He asked what it meant to wake up in a dream,
arms covered with tattoos —
bright and colorful,
elaborately decorated with flowers and birds,
palm leaves and parrots,
reminiscent of a painting by Frida Kahlo —
All manner of flora and fauna!
— on toned muscular arms,
the tanned arms of a youth,
rough-hewn and rippling,
like those of a construction worker
or a common day laborer.

A childhood stutterer, afraid of his father's bad temper,
he spent his youth studying words — a scholar of language,
enlisted into an army's cold war,
on a radio hammering out messages;
middle years managing others' careers instead of his own
till finally this life of a hermit, whittling down to almost ascetic
—
eight or so daily cigarettes, twice-a-day coffee,
a bite of bittersweet chocolate,
his only visible visceral vices.

This man who had spent so much time
out of touch and in conflict with his body —
three times at death's door! —
unaware of the internal wound in his gut
perhaps self-inflicted
like a yogi's intentional self-kill of a vital organ
to welcome it back renewed and reborn.

His life bled away till replenished by four pints of blood
donated by strangers,
arms now attached to lifelines dripping iron.

Perhaps one of his saviors was this strapping dark-maned
youth with tattoos
or maybe he, himself, was now finally celebrating his body,

adoring it with adornment, embracing the cacophony of color
alive all around him,
his heart once again pumping iron-rich blood through his
veins,
carrying the oxygen inhaled so essential to nourish his spirit,
his mind's operation entwined with each breath.

He said he woke up happy and rested,
his only concern was that they would not allow a tattooed
man a Jewish burial,
but then he woke remembering he'd asked to be cremated
so that at last he could be freed of this burden,
freed of his body,
resurrected as spirit.

Roxanne Hoffman runs the small literary press Poets Wear Prada with Jack Cooper. Her elegiac poem "In Loving Memory," illustrated by Edward Odwitt, was released as a chapbook in 2011. Their second collaboration, The Little Entomologist, was published in 2018.

Kathleen Hulser - Night Pours

Night pours over me,
pomegranate and black.
Still widened pupils see in the dark.
The night caller,
his back square as a slice of toast,
admires his long nose and glittering gaze
in a mirror which is blank to me.
Ripples push heat rollers in the air.
Concentrated verbena and swamp mallow scent drifts.
Bunkered in pillows, mesmerized by the theater of dreams,
my limbs sink in perfect bone bowls.
Ancient geothermal forces hint at patterns,
predating homo sapiens
who once thought a mammoth pelt the finest couch.

Kathleen Hulser is a writer, poet, public historian, and activist, and offers poetry at live Open Mics, Poetry Zooms, small press magazines and in various anthologies She was curator at the Museum of the American Gangster, and the NY Transit Museum, and N-Y Historical Society public historian. Press22 Publishing will issue I Don't Write Poetry and You Can't Make Me" in 2024.

Amie Hyson - 'Tis Indeed

'Tis indeed an odd domain
to dwell within; here, on the edge
of the eve of one's own mortality.

Engaged in some strange battle
between suicidal ideation &
the urge to stay alive to live another day;
which takes center stage within an aging psyche,
driven crazy by an unnecessary, leftover
penitent for perfection, disguised as survival
in a world growing ever madder
each year since arrival.

'Tis strange indeed, to
simultaneously seek escape,
while staunchly ensconced in seeking solution,
amidst the seeming dissolution of this
so-called social structure of society,
in which we have collectively agreed to gather
at this time in 3rd dimensional density.

'Tis indeed, interesting to me,
having been freed of that once-born
sense of fear, which previously plagued me,
to come to realize that there will always be
lifelines & timelines left behind to return to,
should it serve my soul & the collective story
of the greater good to do so; but that,
ultimately the choice will be up to me
& that we have ever only been, and always
will be free to choose when, where and if
our souls go forth to be born again.

And yet, 'tis it not also odd indeed,
that right here, in this now, while
down here on the ground,
firmly encased in my current human reality,
when it comes to when & how & if I will
know ahead of time when

my time to go will be;
is still totally beyond
my ability to see…

Amie Hyson lives in Western Massachusetts where she has been writing since 2016. She began facilitating creative writing workshops for women in 2017 and has led numerous workshops for women both in the community & "behind the wall." During the pandemic she began offering weekly online co-ed "Writing Your Recovery" workshop, which is currently on hiatus, but ran weekly for over 4 years. Amie's first collection of poems, "Please Don't Feed the Hungry Ghosts," will be published later this year.

Dane Ince - Moonful

When a nine-year-olds mother
Is murdered in front of them
Shot through a door
The bombs burst the dam
Now the town is flooded
You bring me teenage angst
Like it is the eucharist
Stand on tippy toes
Puff up your chest
Claim to be 5' 8" when you are 5'-7"
The rich famous podcaster
The wanna-be poet ah nostalgia
Claim lights of Poe
Kerouac
Without a single drop of Rain
I grow weary of my need to help
More than I
Are weary of me as well
I do not come to you for a solution
The one who rescues is the one who needs saving
I wish you would let me take care
It is a need
Testicular assertion of manhood
Comes across as embarrassing
Personality poison
Every self-absorbed one
Perhaps the best
Are considering that path
Over there
Far away from coodies
Self pity

The lost
The rest
I am
Have have no answers
I find no peace
In this mournful life
Full of eclipsing moons

Heartache
I had a life before
And Before
And before
As dry as sandy dirt road
I am fresh out of ideas
Why anyone would want
A lost thread
Paper clips
Dust in the corner
At some point it is futile to ask for more
He said," See that shimmer?"
I think sometimes I see things that no one else does
Feeling flat
Crickets complain after dusk
Fireflies
Milky Way
Whisper of what was crumbles
Cats complain and I do not understand
That I do not understand
But a while a go
He read his poem about the wheel
Mumble through flame red ginger beard
The kitchen denizen traded in his good humor white jacket

Hounds tooth slacks
For standard issue beat black
And willow long haired company hands held walking north on the avenue
The artist stride came with confidence
Of the once diffident dish washer's snear
Ah nostalgia
Wretched food poisoning
I will try to keep it to myself
But big spit will not be denied
And before I had a life.
A life I had before
The drawer is waiting for me to empty it
Waiting to be
It is terrible
I love to watch the fake aquarium on the roku

On the cgi tv
Know so many may not have the peace
Watching tropical fish swim
In the warm cgi water
Waiting to be
The drawer is waiting for me to empty it
A life I had before
And before I had a life.
But big spit will not be denied
I will try to keep it to myself
Wretched food poisoning
ah nostalgia
Of the once diffident dish washer's snear
The artist stride came with confidence
And willow long haired company hands held walking north on the avenue

For standard issue beat black
Hounds tooth slacks
The kitchen denizen traded in his good humor white jacket
Mumble through flame red ginger beard
He read his poem about the wheel
But a while a go
That I do not understand
Cats complain and I do not understand
Whisper of what was crumbles
Milky Way
Fireflies
Crickets complain after dusk
Feeling flat
I think sometimes I see things that no one else does
He said," See that shimmer?"
At some point it is futile to ask for more
Dust in the corner
Paper clips
A lost thread
Why anyone would want
I am fresh out of ideas
As dry as sandy dirt road
And before
And Before

I had a life before
Heartache
Full of eclipsing moons
In this mournful life
I find no peace
I am
Have have no answers

The rest
The lost
Self-pity
Far away from coodies
Over there
Are considering that path
Perhaps the best
Every self-absorbed one
Personality poison
Comes across as embarrassing
Testicular assertion of manhood
It is a need
I wish you would let me take care
The one who rescues is the one who needs saving
I do not come to you for a solution
Are weary wary of me as well
More than I
I grow weary of my need to help
Without a single drop of Rain
Kerouac
Claim lights of Poe
The wanna-be poet
The rich famous podcaster
Claim to be 5' 8" when you are 5'-7"
Puff up your chest
Stand on tippy toes
Like it is the eucharist
You bring me teenage angst

Now the town is flooded
The bombs burst the dam
Shot through a door
Is murdered in front of them

When a nine-year-olds mother is shot in front of her kids
It is terrible
This hunger moon

Dane Ince is an internationally published poet, named Beat Poet Laureate for California, and hosts a weekly open mic- Time to Arrive, and founder of EYEPUBLISHEWE.

Larry Jaffe - Poetry In The Lost And Found

words leak out from ancestral homes
the holy grail of coffeehouses
that lighted our path with verse

these holy locals provided succor
to the word carrying voices that lit our way
from the darkness and confines of the past

we pay homage to the poets who read there
performed their work to hip crowds
who did not know they were stylish

ancestor's words changed the face of the earth
poets who claimed anonymity rather than fame
snapped their fingers to the jazz like tomb

where the words began
and thoughts bloomed
in silent rectitude

poetry so lost in the confines heard only by
a selection of minions
poetry in the lost and found

Larry Jaffe
Poet/Writer
Human Rights Activist
Lifetime New Generation Beat Poet Laureate
Poet in Residence Jack Kerouac House in St. Petersburg
www.lgjaffe.com

Allan Johnston - The Air Museum
(Soviet Dream Hitch Hike Poem, 1989)

A fictionalization of an actual dream,
spoken to a figure from a novel
based on a real person, long since dead,
occurring in a land that has disappeared.
A poem of the Reagan-Bush era.

I'm thinking of you today, Moriarty,
because last night I was on the road
in my dream,
far from the plastic plant
where I work, between Ulsk and Minsk,

eighty cents to my name, a red-inked passport
with huge murky thumbprints under the seal
of the Great Soviet, and HITCHHIKE stamped
in Cyrillic under "mode of transport,"

showing my ignorance -- I never knew
them Russians owned cars: maybe Cosmonaut wives
or the hot bubalinskis of party dons --
do they raise fingers
to give the bird
before leaning down
on golf-tee door locks,
eyes lost in sunglasses,
heads in bright curlers
under their socialist
Babushkas?
Fifty
miles and Moscow no closer -- Vermont-style
farms laze under crabapple trees
on meadows that gently slope up hills
to purple mountains' majesties
on these roads
that don't
exist:

all this scenery and I'm getting hungry.
Eighty cents isn't much good in Russia
anyway, there's no Safeway
and no one knows
a dime from St. Christopher.

That's what it's like in a place where people
talk like "is beink" and forests grow thick:
the ground now damper, the cedars feather
to Catherine the Great (NOW
knowing I'm dreaming):
icons and Czars
pop up in glens
and heavy gold frames
surround copulas
trimmed with bears and two-headed eagles,
and drapes hang down to the footlights:

Ou suis-je? I ask, wrong tongued. Grazhdanka
Pulzhalsta, the tour guide, badge and white blouse,
doesn't answer. I walk through forests,
touch the imaginary walls

where courtyards blossom and corridors lead
to cool green wooden throne rooms.
I try German. She speaks in Russian.
She leans on a case of immaculate bracelets,
inspecting the ornate shivers of stones
and silver light rippling like birds through trees:

Ah shrine of woes, fable of Ludwig
von Gottseidank
who penned the Märchen,
told of the secret
storms of reason
in times when trees
lived with history.
The grove I had entered
"war nicht ein Musée
des beaux arts" -- so schrieb
der Herr -- "aber doch

das richtige Musée
der Luft."   For thus fall
Phenomena,
Dean,
the telling of tales,

the odd combine of labor and flight
in what I do at work all day
in city rebeautification
sending cockroaches to paradise,
the dismal death and sudden rebirth
of roaches that crawl out of plastic bottles
I drop in the meltdown containers, repeating
life as dreams repeat in me;

dreams that flower from nothingness;
fantastic museums out of the air!
Gone from the woods so long they could be
Samarkand for all I know,
I live in a city, in the USA,
Dean, I know myself between sleep
and death doing things I won't remember
so I can eat, then going home to sleep:

that's why I dream of the air museum
popping out of the blue, Dean,
a history of strategic defense,
system I use when pinstriped suits
show up on the cover of Time or Pravda
so real
you know who's boss:

I dream tales out of the air, Dean,
knowing tomorrow I'll be on the job
just as you'll be somewhere on
your highway of lost
tomorrows;

there's no need to worry: the whole shebang
of life continues --
the world slowly spins

out of imagination,
a punctured
plastic
coke bottle
bleeding.

Allan Johnston has published work in Poetry, Poetry East, Rattle, Rhino, and other journals. His poetry books and chapbooks are Tasks of Survival, 1996, Northport, 2010, Departures, 2013, Contingencies, 2015m In a Window, 2018, and Sable and Selected Poems, 2022. His translations and co-translations of poems have appeared in Ezra, Metamorphosis, Mayday Magazine, and Transference.

Catherine Katey Johnson -
*Memories, Suite (in four parts)

Victim

Mowed down
then back toward the house
and down again.
Clipped,
raked it over,
blown and dried so
hard to bag it
scattered by the hope of air.

Did the lawn,
the sheets,
uniform
meals and yet you'd have me
beg for lovemaking.

Tender of the children
minding them and home.
victim of early marriage.
Twenty years to recover myself.

Survivor

I don't want to go back.
Please, call him, I told the neighbor,
Mom said to have you call my brother
to come and break it up.

I remember the gray pitcher
shaped like that powdered drink mix.
smiling pitcher -- held lemony goodness and so much ice
so cold it sweat.
That one glass,
this one aluminum,
so it dented when it hit his temple.
She was trying to keep him off

trying to avoid his hand.
He restrained her too hard and I ran out
when he raised the cast-iron skillet up over her.

Participant
Single years.
Disco-functional
people going from bed
to worse.

Leisure suites and
casual sex to match
three pieces and move on.

Victor

And I went to the movies.
My first job was there
at fourteen
already sneaking TV on for two years straight
in the dark silence while others slept
searching a black and white screen
for Midnight
Moonlight Matinee
Night Owl Movie
life beyond
the doom of constant arguments.
Trying to imagine what it was like to be directed
to live happily
knowing only black and white
his version, her side,
right, wrong, trial, why bother.
open and shut and nobody budge
at the bell, the round always going to the muscle.

There was this actor
in Cinema-color
and I loved to say his name
Victor
Mature.

*This poem was published in the literary journal, "The Woman," New Plains Review, Volume 3, Number 1, College of Liberal Arts, University of Central Oklahoma, Edmond, Oklahoma.

It was also published in South Korea, by Sung, Printing America, Inc.

Catherine Katey Johnson
Award-winning Author; Woody Guthrie poet and Beat poet living in Cushing, OK. Her Resting Soil and Fifty Shades of Gray Hair, a tangled collection, don't have numbered pages because in Oklahoma, women don't count. Her works are in many anthologies. Her spoof, MAGNUM FARCE was a deadCenter Film Festival screenplay finalistand THE HANDLER won the Oklahoma Horror Film

Alex S. Johnson - Denatured: The Triumph of Eco-Snuff with a wave of the Gregor feelers to Pixie Bruner

I
Night glimmer of structural surreal
as the bee-eyes of the dark moon saints
stab with their optic knives
A thriving colony pierced down through the riverbed
biofilm sprocketed, mountains and wound-down tunnels
running red
That wiggles feelers in the feels
fur, feather, to-scale models of the reptile brain with bed hair
In the grim boudoir
where the crimson king reigns forevermore
Tis pity she's a whore

II
Circle saws of angel
arche-light wings majestic
That blew through the crass ceiling right to the powers
of the air
that blew like sainted sinners on their knees on Victorian
cobblestoned streets
Bloody spunked Eco-snuff queens
erupt a cinema fountain of dreams

III
Smeared raptures of rent boys haunted by
the ghosts of disease
Blackmailing lords and ladies
of the alley oop hep cat circuit boards
Opium tidal waves consume the scholar
buried in the endless armchair
HIs automaton double still drumming
its name through the vault of the stars

IV
The snot-like vestigial shreds on bones of
the dead museum
Carrion crowns of poverty
immersing suns at the bottom of the greenmucked sea

Where Aleph the cryptic mirror gleams
snatched flashes of the yellow king's barbarity
Where seaweed chokes piratical eyes
and the tyrannical maidens burst through waves of multicol-
ored wreckage
Weighed down and watching
the bubbles slip from her tender cropped lips
His throat slit and
dying violet the flag of evening
Her dark hair plunging into
limit experience of the jacked-in Goblin market

V
Where cruelty of the churchbell book and candle
rears a skeletal mast on the bones of the ship of screams
Darkness has a specific gradient
sliced down and off through interlaced black ribbons
That score through the bared breasts
and raised skirts of Piccadilly harlots
bearing candles that wind down the scarlet streets
of immensity
Her hunger blares like discordant music
drums through her guts, percussive smackdown in thegrave

VI
Wheels of angels fused with demons roll across the sky
while we're all waiting for the Gabardine swine to fly
Heavens, it seems we are polluted
and a really nasty carapace yolks in our meat!
The Queen of the vampires is quite stylized
and covets all your eyes
Skitter of guitars in dubstepchildren shudder
gorekids have at themselves and one another
Heaven helps those in the mirror-hell of selves
warped silver costumes adorning the ghouls
with fashion's smile
A drink of sweet wine and wild cleavage
yanks into place the bloated, oozing map of atrocities

VII
Dramatis personae none gratify
leaving the pearl of great piss on the mistress of woes
She of the nimble fingers and toes
Her descending tongue ferrets the abyss
Whittled bliss in starlight
hacked mind weapons burn through systems
Punked gash in all five dimensions
clench of the shield they bore you out on
The language of tombs is always rehearsed
like the triumph of death on nature's perverse
The Earth moves, creatures, gutted, crisped creators
ripple through the wombs of the unearthed.

Alex S. Johnson is an author, music journalist and publisher currently residing in Sacramento, California. H is upcoming anthology, The Junk Merchants 2: A Literary Tribute to William S. Burroughs, contains contributions by such esteemed authors as Ron Whitehead, Poppy Z Brite and Caitlin Kiernan.

karlostheunhappy - I know this game

i know this game:
brautigan's 'All Watched Over by the Loving Machines of Grace'
or when ginsberg demanded to know, America, 'when can I go
into the supermarket and buy what I need with my good looks?'
oh allen, blakean, one of whitman's wild children
how you farmed stanzas, whole litanies of sunflowers
a reader's feast –
yet me, myself and I;
we're all so goddamn ugly w/21century loneliness
all i do is sit around all day lamenting dead dream of the DDR –

sigh
sigh knowing the moon shines richer than the killer coin
that the flowers in the litter will rise
that their day will be unholy in its sweet holiness

coins only for the eyes of the dead
of the old guard
as we pay our way in rich rituals on dreammachineplans & the
exquisite corpse
share the new remarkable

i know this game:
the reality dream as it should be
you know, all that smiling love, cultless
capitalism relegated to laughing stock
filed back there, way back there, with the mumbling flat-earthers

Karlostheunhappy hails from the warm dark sheltering shade of the Forest of Dean in England and is International Beat Poet Laureate (England). His first collection, OBLIVION followed by FLUX (both on Gloomy for Pleasure). He is the editor at BeatSurreal and his work has featured in numerous anthologies and Beatdom, it (International Times) and the Broken Spine presses Beat collection, 'After Hours: Beat Culture Made New'. Find out more at gloomyforpleasure.com and follow on facebook.com/karlostheunhappy

Eliot Katz - To the Vegetable Aisle

Under refrigerated water spray all looks healthy,
romaine, red & green, boston bib, watercress--
        how do you choose a lettuce?
How to know which of you has natural soil's nutrients intact?
Hey arugula! Why haven't I seen you here before?
Who let those prepackaged sick leaves in the door?
There's plenty broccoli bunches, no ketchup--
        at least the Reagan/Bush era is over!
Which squash has more vitamin A?
Spaghetti or butternut?
        Would one of you please raise your label?
Speak up! Which of you has been microwaved?
Who here likes Creamy Italian?
Who's not afraid of the juicer's steel blades?
Brussel sprouts and red cabbage, settle your price wars
        peacefully.
Chestnuts, are you a vegetable now?
Ah, tofu, you are the cure for famine & carnivorism.
No wonder the U.S. wants
        your French soybean subsidies cut!
How juicy these ripe Jersey tomatoes
        lulling me for an illusory moment
                this really could be a garden state.

Wait a minute now! Why isn't this aisle as well lit
        as the candy bar section?
Why is a Mars bar cheaper than a bag of spinach?
Doesn't it cost more to grow a candy bar?
When a six-year old child I remember watching
        a professional wrestler described
                as having a "cauliflower" ear.
Cauliflower, it was 20 years
before I could look at you again.
Actually, for a long time in childhood I refused
        to eat vegetables.
It was a way of rebelling I think.
Later, I substituted alcohol for not eating vegetables.
Now I welcome you radical & mostly sober

escarole & chicory
Now kale, now garlic, now red peppers & parsley.

Peas & green beans,
who will protect you from being canned
        and frozen to death?
Without values of internationalism & democratic accountability
        in all public institutions
                who will safeguard the diversity?
Who will protect us from irradiation & pesticide?
Who will assure the right to organize?
Who sets transnational standards of minimum wage,
eco-health,
        & safe working conditions?
Who will make sure hyper-technology doesn't take over?
After a right-wing tide, who will remineralize your soil?
Who will assure access to your aisle for all?
Who will apologize for bumping my cart into shoppers
        while writing this poem?
Sleep tight, don't let the bacteria bite--
feed the struggle for another night.

Eliot Katz

Called "another classic New Jersey bard" by the late Allen Ginsberg, Eliot Katz is the author of seven books of poetry, including Love, War, Fire, Wind and Unlocking the Exits, as well as a prose book, The Poetry and Politics of Allen Ginsberg. Katz, whose late mother was a Holocaust survivor, has worked for many years as an activist for a wide range of peace and social-justice causes. He currently lives in Hoboken, NJ and his website is at www.eliotkatzpoetry.com

Joe Kidd - Lawmakers/Lawbreakers

over time 9 generations justice crying waiting
"what of me, my broken limb
the painful wound upon my heart
the silver scar across my wrist"
do you believe that I am here, and that I look to find a truth
beyond the dark and clouded surface
of a room beyond a door revolving,
circling carnivores grinning
I'll eat you for lunch, I'll set you free
I'll give you anything you want
I'll provide the circuitry
something smoking in the kitchen
beyond the tempered blood stained glass
where your fingerprints were found beyond,
unreasonable unspoken doubt
give me a chance to prove you wrong
a history of cutting blades, across a landscape in upheaval
the model citizen, a home grown hometown clown
but you made this law, you made it happen,
you created a secret desire
your struggle amounts to a call to arms,
a city burning with holy fire
it was not me, I did not do it, I did not walk the sacred path
a mountain too high for one such as I,
who would rather read the book
than actually look, down at a valley from the highest peak
you see, I am too weak, to even speak, a word to cause a
fleeting moment
enter now my testimony, of tears, of sorrow, and regret
before I forget to wipe you out, put you away
rest you in piec-es in a body bag
how could I redeem my disloyalty,
my unfaithfulness to such a power
it's just a needle, you won't feel a thing
now go to sleep and think of mommy
here is a napkin for when you start to drool

the snake may slither up the pole
to heal the sick with hollow recitation

if the page were blank it would offer more
to comfort a failing nation
let her make her laws both day and night
I will fall asleep and in my slumber
I will dream of ways to ignore and break them
into paragraphs that the comedians steal
but humor is not the true intention,
rather to serve up domination
before my morning feet hit the floor,
I have enacted every crime
they have made it easy, made it necessary, and unavoidable
the purpose was to make me honorable and vulnerable

guilty as charged
I heard those words before
were they of the baptist in the sanctuary
the physician with her sharpened pen
the dark robed shadow with the blackened tongue
a language dead for a thousand years
spoken here behind a curtain
a capability purchased and privileged
seek not and you shall never find
the stone under which the key was hidden
where the philosopher sat to drink the wine

yes it was sweet, a colorful toxin
the umbilical cord, torn away
eternal, natural, human, divine
before I knew it, I was gone
on the run from the invisible infraction
the ghost of "justice" a step behind
and now invincible, I stand before you
graduate/veteran of trial and error, battle worn, victorious
"there ain't no speed limit, there ain't no law"
that I can't break
with one hand tied behind my back
and a rope around my neck
my brothers and sisters have all disappeared
locked up, put away, for the rest of their life, or mine
now you can brag, and you can rant, and you can go to hell
tell me all the wonders you have performed

while living in your see through prison
no one cares, it does not matter,
there is only one world
and you are not in it

I heard the crack, the fractured skull
suddenly the great law is obeyed
funny how easily small minds are changed

Joe Kidd - Michigan Beat Poet Laureate 2022-2024.
Michigan Rock & Roll Legends Hall Of Fame.
Lifelong working/touring poet, songwriter, activist for
world peace, social justice, cultural diversity,
personal freedom, political and economic equality for all.

Patti Barker Kierys - Silence To Listen

Sitting beneath the maple tree
blazing colors all around
rustling leaves in the breeze
blue sky and puffy clouds
let the beauty abound

Listen and let the silence come in
listen in silence to truly hear
breathe and let it settle within
silence awakens the inner spirit

Listen to the whispering winds
answers arrive from deep within
awakening dreams lying dormant
amazed and surprised yet received
as the silence begins again

Silence lets stress evaporate
no worries can penetrate
hearing that tiny voice
never in doubt or alone

Leave nature's sacred space
sense all the wonder of it
visit often this special tree
for moments of peace
silence when in need

Patti Barker Kierys is an award-winning artist, Reiki Master Teacher, author, poet and photographer. Her creativity can be seen in her poems, paintings, collage, photography and inspirational messages. She writes for the international organization Reiki Rays. After retiring 50 years working in law, she began writing poetry. She can be reached at pmkierys@att.net and on Facebook - Patti Barker Kierys

Debbie Tosun Kilday - When Twilight Comes

When twilight comes
As shadows start to fall
My mind will start to wander

Back to the days
When I had nothing
Nothing but a thought
To get out
Move out into the light

Hunger makes you
Want to anguish
In disappointment
But your determination
Makes you fight to survive

Instead of wallowing
Feeling bewildered
Overwhelmed & hopeless

You rally
With strength
Using your intelligence
Kindness
Empathy
Things that cannot
Be stolen

You defeat your situation
By reinventing yourself
Each time

When twilight comes
I won't be prepared
To accept it

Instead
I will lay in the sun
Warming my soul

As if I will shine
Forever

Debbie Tosun Kilday is a Beat Poet, writer, award winning author, nature photographer, artist and founder/owner of the National Beat Poetry Foundation, Inc., it's Festivals, New Generation Beat Publications, BeatLife Magazine, and Kilday Krafts. Debbie is a Connecticut, native and resident.

Tom Lagasse - If Not Now, When?
For Greta Thunberg & Sophia Kianni

In a more innocent
but equally turbulent
time Gary Snyder wrote:

“Perhaps one should
not talk (Or write)
too much

About the wild
world: it may be
that it embarrasses

Other animals to have
attention called
upon them.”[1]

Fearing their
embarrassment
(and ours)

We have kept
a silent vigil
as one by one,

Like ancestors,
they depart us.
Is now it too late

To speak or should
we forever hold
our peace

As we witness
humanity’s
toxic marriage -

Its true place
in the cosmos
and the romance

Of dominion,
which ambition
cannot divorce.

The silent witnesses
red wolves, Florida
panthers, manatees

Loggerhead
Sea Turtles,
California condors,

Mississippi gopher
frogs, San Joaquin
kit foxes, Franklin's

Bumblebees, black-footed
ferrets, and Lange's
metalmark butterflies

Are endangered by silence.
Their names read like
a roll call of the dead

Strangled by the hands
of terrorists and
the pandemic of greed

Where the people,
and the government,
of the so-called most

Powerful nation
did not want to
draw attention

To their lack
Of love, lack
of shame, and

Lack of wildness
in not saying enough
before extinction.

[1] Gary Snyder. "The Practice of the Wild." Gary Snyder Reader. Pg. 180

Tom Lagasse's poetry has appeared in The Silver Birch Poetry Series, Freshwater Literary Journal, The Eunoia Review, and in numerous anthologies. He will be one of the 2924 Writers in Residence at the Edwin Way Teale House at Trail Wood. He lives in Bristol, CT.

Scott Laudati - Thus Passes the Glory of the World

I've seen Kentucky through this windshield
three times since January.
In winter Nathan drives
and we're still tired from the night in St. Louis.
In spring I drive and I remember a story about Whitman
heading our way before turning south.
In summer it's Tohm's turn and we stop in Wheeling
to see where the stagecoaches ran out of road,
before the bridge was built,
and now it has collapsed.
The grass is never blue but the river's always brown.
I haven't read a book written by a stranger in over a year.
Every time I get into a car there's a destination.
It's not like walking.
I always know where I'm going.
On Sunday we rob a grocery store and get out
with three burritos and a six pack.
Tohm is taking us fast through the Allegheny Tunnel
and I use my lighter to open two beers.
Will we sleep better tonight?
Who lives inside these highway trailers?
There are red lights appearing before us like deer eyes
wide and lost under a setting sun.
I don't say slow down.
We can sleep forever rubbed on this asphalt.
We can dream in sentences buried beneath it.

Scott Laudati is the author of Play the Devil, Camp Winapooka and others. He runs Bone Machine from his apartment in NYC with his dog, Josie. Visit him anywhere @ ScottLaudati

Christen Lee - Everything Except

I carry a wound
the size of a city
tucked deep inside
my jacket pocket—
written on pages
folded neatly inside
my shirt's breast pocket.

Skin of paper,
history of letters,
it's easier to house the heart

outside the body

where I live in ledgers,
scribble epitaphs,
dwell in memorial fields.
I carry a graveyard
of verse upon my chest,

ripped-page planners
of futures forsaken.
I'll coin a clever phrase
for every heartbroken
ending

worn upon my lips,
blood red,
smudged by Poseidon's kiss,
an ocean of salt and sadness,
deep blue.
I convince myself that
it's better this way,

swimming circles around
dead-ends,
yesterday's hopes
a sunken ballast.

I am a sailor wrecked at sea.
Can you hear me?

I carry my secrets
closer than a heartbeat,
telling you everything
except what‘s buried beneath.

Christen Lee is a family nurse practitioner in Cleveland, Ohio. Her writing has been featured in Rue Scribe, The Write Launch, Aurora, Humans of the World, Sad Girls Club, New Generation Beats Anthology, Encephalon, In Parentheses, The Elevation Review, and Moot Point among others.

Mark Lipman - Third Populist Manifesto
for Lawrence Ferlinghetti

The sons of another
Whitman awake
Retake the word
Retake the song
There's no time now
for sleeping till noon
in your shuttered rooms
There's no time now
as New York crumbles
beneath our feet
under the trampling
of a nation of sheep
as Kabul is wiped
off the map
as the Palestinian
follows in the footsteps
of the Native American

gone with the echoes
of a thousand mother's cries
everyone asking "Why?"

Not for freedom
Not for democracy
But for a new kingdom
ruled by philanthropy

Yes, blood is thicker
than water
but not as thick
as oil

How many must still be killed
to keep the drills alive?

Where are the new Ginsbergs
the new Dylans
the voices of a new generation

with their cut-up jeans
and backpacks?

Where are all the great
minds of today
Still roaming their
dark alleyways?

Yes, Ferlinghetti is still alive
but so too is Dick Cheney
The usurpers are still
in the House
And all the voices
remain silent

How many Kyotos
must be rejected?
How many Johannesburgs
over-ruled by a party of one?
How many rulers selected
and promises broken

before we stand up
and speak out
and take back
what should be ours
guaranteed by birth?

Whitman's wild children
are all alive and well
So put down your glasses
and pick up your pens
Get on your buses
all going "Further"
And let your voices
be heard.

Mark Lipman, founder of the press Vagabond, the Culver City Book Festival, the Elba Poetry Festival; winner of the 2015 Joe Hill Labor Poetry Award; the 2016 International Latino Book Award and the 2023 L'Alloro di Dante (Dante's Laurel - Italy), a writer, poet, multi-media artist, activist and author of fourteen books, began as the writer-in residence at the world famous Shakespeare and Company in Paris, France (2002-2003). He has worked closely with legendary poets, Lawrence Ferlinghetti and Jack Hirschman on many projects. He's the host and foreign correspondent for the radio program, Poetry from Around the World for Poets Café on KPFK 90.7FM Los Angeles. Mark uses poetry to connect communities to the greater social justice issues, while building consciousness through the spoken word.

Sheila Lowe-Burke - The Great Separator

Pain, the great separator
Physical, mental, emotional
Hasty withdrawal, a lonely retreat.
Seeking sanctuary, a bit of respite
The question why, the great Tormenter.
What is the cause, what can be done
Will they understand when I can't attend
What did I do right or wrong
How can I, how could I, have fixed this?

And what is so holy about suffering?
Is there any Redemption here?
Perhaps righteous time spent in prayer
Arduous, long, lonely hours, moment to momentary pain
Visions of Jesus, angels, and others
Departed loved ones. Hopes dashed, faith renewed.

A moment of joy when pain lifts
Deepened compassion, sometimes the gift.
Mourning time lost and gatherings missed
Friends who moved on, lovers and spouses
Solitary confinement, lost opportunities
Such disappointment, faltered beginnings.

Try again. Take one step. Write one verse.
Eat a bite. Keep it down. Do the therapy.
Maintain the treatments. Take the meds. Rest. Rest. Rest.
Renewed determination. Repeat.

Lying here, on the edge of the bed,
Of the world, on the ledge of sanity,
Nearing the verge of leaving humanity.
Telling myself, it'll be alright. Will it, though?
Time will tell. Yet, it isn't hell that troubles me
Only lies and hypocrisy.
But, in this head and in this heart
Determined again, to make a new start,
And hide the pain within my art.

Sheila Lowe-Burke Dr, hc, Intl Union Peace Federation. Univ of Pikeville,Ky, liberal arts theology. Spring Arbor Univ, Detroit, business mgmt. Minister of Culture & Poetry, State of Birland, NA. Royal Amb Elite Arab Creative Union. World Figure 50 Memorable Women of North Am,Forbes Mexico 2024. CEO of JKSB Media, LLC. Inductee, MI Rock-n-Roll Legends Hall of Fame. Touring concert recording artist, speaker, poet, author, lyricist, vocal duo joekiddandsheilaburke.com

PD Lyons - My Daughter Aged Seven Asks

What happens when you die Daddy?
What really happens after you die Dad?

Am I afraid of death?
Afraid of not being me anymore?
Am I afraid of life?
Afraid of not knowing answers?
Growing old?
Forgetting?

My mommy my daddy. Grandma Grandpa Aunts & uncles.
How they looked where they died – hospitals wakes funerals
What they taught me?
Names of dogs, my first cat,
Cards, poker, slapjack, war, set-back, cribbage, 31, solitaire, rummy.
Smoking: corn silk, Pall Mall, Kent, Old Gold, Lucky Strike, Viceroy Marlboro, Mores.
TV: channel 8, ABC, Superman, Twilight Zone, Avengers, Popeye, Lone Ranger, Roy Rogers, Rifleman, Sugarfoot , Captain Kangaroo (how to tie my shoes), Bunny- rabbit, Mr. Moose, Tom Terrific, Sonny Fox, Sandy Becker, Ranger Andy, Outer Limits, Bugs what's up doc Bunny (all I know about classical music) and oh that mighty mighty mouse and the farmer and the mice (made before sound all action to a can-can score), Zorro, Robin Hood, Paladin, Seaview, Sea Hunt, Flipper, Twenty Mule Team Death Valley Days.

Stateline potato chips, Mr Salty pretzels, Oreos, Drake's cakes, Cracker Jack, sandwiches, deli grinders, first sip sting- my- nose Knickerbocker Beer, Hires real root beer, Diamond ginger ale, real mayonnaise, sour pickles, Pepsi Cola, cream off the top of the milk bottle.

Big giant glittering maniacal magical Christmas, and the baby, baby Jesus in his little wooden manger. Easter bunnies, Easter baskets, vinegary coloured eggs. Halloween, store bought costumes, pillow cases full of trick or treating treats.

Songs my mother whistled in the garden, all the flowers she taught me names of, the birds she always fed, the pets she always had Nietzsche, Fritz, Simon, Suki, Dulcinea, Heidi, Beau, Nietzsche II, Terry, Frisky, Penny, Mamma Kitty, Tuffy, Tasha.

My father's chess set, going fishing, making models together: black bear & cub, USS Missouri "big Mo", making us sawn and sanded swords at his work bench, heavy iron wrenches, hammers I could hardly lift, picks that weighed more than I did.

Cub Scouts, baseball, sledding on the golf course, going up the bank, down the rock fort, up the rez, taste of snow, scent of autumn bright sun on brown leaves orange & yellow & up to your knees holding hands with mom walking down peach orchard hill to glimpse a sight of JFK waving as he went by on his way to Hartford.

Roger Maris as a rookie my first time at the major league his first Yankee game, Mickey Mantle, Whitey Ford and oh yeah Yogi Berea! Summer vacations, going to the ocean - five kids all are- we- there- yet packed into the Chevy station wagon when Connecticut to Maine really took forever...

My daughter loves the sea
We don't live near it
Sometimes get to visit
Dancing in and out the surf
Up and down the Dogs Bay regardless of the weather.
And maybe it's not so bad to forget?
make space for right now
stop so much looking back.

And maybe it can be that way with death?
not so bad, letting go of all this me?
making space for something new?
But I've a strong ego
Tuff as nails
A Buddha's nightmare
Veteran of all kind of wars.

Maybe that's the equation:
stronger the ego – stronger the fear?

Love is not an answer.
Love is a response to all those unanswerable questions.

Not knowing anything, I love.
The more answers I don't have?
The more I feel my own true love.

I don't know what really happens when we die honey
But I do know how much I love you ~

20 Jan 09 for Morgan Macha

PD Lyons born and raised in the USA. Since 1998 has resided in Ireland. Lyons received Mattatuck College Award for Outstanding Achievement in Poetry, Bachelor of Science with honours from Teikyo Post University. Outright winner of the annual erbacce-press International Poetry Competition for 2019. The work of PD Lyons has appeared in many formats throughout the world

Joe Maldonado - Lady in the Water

In the undulating harbor under overcast skies,
our lady stands tall,
a beacon of hope for one and all.
Yet beneath her stoic face and copper crown,
Lies a heart that's heavy, a silent breakdown.

She's watched the seasons come and go,
felt the city's heartbeat, fast and slow.
But now, she senses a change in the air,
A nation's discourse, tinged with despair.

Where once stood unity, strong and sure,
division's shadow now creeps over the shores.
Her torch still burns with a steadfast flame,
While the ideals it represents, lay broken and maimed.

She weeps not for herself, but for those seeking to be free,
For the huddled masses yearning to breathe.
The image of freedom, once so pure and bright,
Now clouded by day, obscured by night.

Still, in this sadness, she finds resolve,
For the spirit of independence, she must absolve.
Standing as a symbol, firm and true,
A reminder of what we must renew.

Let her cries be a call,
To mend the cracks and tear down walls,
To get back to fulfilling those long deferred dreams,
How can we dare name her Liberty
And forget what it means?

Joe Maldonado is a writer from New York. His latest poetry collection, The Beautiful Ugliness of Being (Alien Buddha Press, 2023) is a winner of the Literary Titan and The Bookfest awards. He has published two other poetry books and his work can be found in numerous anthologies. Follow him @joemaldonado81.

Patricia Martin - Secrets of the Nymphs

Maybe she knew the secrets of the nymphs
because she was one
Knew the ripe life, the heated language of lovers
thoughtlessly, fearlessly, slipping into her desires
embracing experiences
during misty afternoons lost to trickling rain and fingertips
when the wind was howling and knocking at the window in unison with cries
on the satin moss of the forest floor witnessed by crows
in the backseat of a father's borrowed car
among the undulating waves of pure blue Caribbean seas
the furtive isolation of a Manhattan hotel room
before rush hour
during the darkest of nights entwined in the softest of beds
or anytime
when seduction aroused and beckoned
and she thought, "Why not?"

She was never taught
never instructed
She owned the magic
She wove the magic
singing the siren song
for those who would listen and hear
those aching to be beguiled
mesmerized
for an hour
or two
or three
with the Muse
who would kiss them soundly
before saying goodbye

Patricia Martin - State of Connecticut Beat Poet Laureate Patricia Martin is an author, poet, performer/actor, and freelance writer/communications professional who has been featured at numerous venues, festivals, on radio and television, and published in various periodicals and anthologies. Martin is the author of six nonfiction books as well as the poetry collection In Venice I Could Sing and Is Love So Fickle, a haiku chapbook. More information can be found at www.patriciamartin.com.

Ángel L. Martínez 1 June 2024 -Maestro Marshall Allen: 100 Arrivals Serenading the Earth

I once told you how you have, on a warm June night,
I saw Saturn in the sky, sensing the spirit of Sun Ra shooting straight back.

You told me how so often you too would stare at Saturn,
wondering, hoping that you are best on the legacy
of Sun Ra and his Arkestra where you took on the lead.

We all knew you'd make your 100th arrival day.
Was it destiny or was it Alter Destiny?
What matters is that you have firmly placed your star
among the spaceways we must travel.

I remember my first time in the presence of the Arkestralive,
at the bandshell in Central Park in Summer 1987.
I saw you and your companions do your thing
I saw glimpses of what can be in all of you,
up to your traditional march around the stage.

Today, you shine on the stage as the sage of interstellar voyagers.
Time again to share with Earth the wonder of imagination,
our most powerful weapon to let out the truth.

As you once told me in congratulations,
"On up, straight ahead!"
On up, straight ahead, Maestro! It's the time!

Ángel L. Martínez is a poet and musician on the road throughout the Northeast. He is working on a new book of poems. His work appears on SoundCloud and Bandcamp.

John C. Massett - Between two Deltas

I walk between two deltas
Not like the triangular area where a major river
Divides into several smaller parts that usually flow into a larger body of water.
I walked down Baldwin Avenue on a hot day
And I noticed two Delta Gas Stations
One right across the street from the other one
I thought it was funny
If one was full up
Do a K-Turn and hit up the other one
Fill the tank
Of the motorized carriages
We all use now to take ourselves
To places we need to go
Wherever we just feel like going
To get away for a while
Change it up

Over time, both went under
The metaphorical river bloated up
And swallowed the Deltas once again
As easily as they had risen, they sank
Gates were put up
Massive machines rolled
Everything was drained
Tanks exhumed from the ground
Buildings bulldozed
The land covered with sand
They stayed that way behind chain link
For many months

One day, construction began on the site of the left Delta
A large condominium
So we locals can one day say
To the new settlers
"I bought gas where you sleep now"
"I had my car where you make dinner every night"
"I got my oil changed where you change your baby's diapers"
The other former Delta site is a home for wayward cats it

seems
Someone feeds them
And they lounge in the vacant lot all day

Gas stations are going down these days
An old Getty station I used to patronize
Has become a 7-11
And that's surprising
And I smile that I can get junk food late
But the landscape has changed
And we have to change with it
Or just deal with it
As we grow older
The planet shifts

John C. Massett is a writer and poet that has been performing at open mics in the tri-state area for the past 25 years. In 2003 he self-published a chapbook of poetry called Procrastinating Ass. In 2008, with some friends, John started a free literary magazine called Afterword which focused on poetry, short story, and art. His latest chapbook Good Luck with Your Future Endeavors published (he printed copies) in 2021.

Amy Christine Matus - Hot Hooting

cold as a warm tone
her blushing secrecy
Heats curiosity like
a roll in bed spirals curl
Colors of Sweet
drumming like a beat poet
cheering Jiminy Cricket!
   ...eye-rolling
Lallygagging ...all that boogie like
Coo does this silly boy
Caw did that lady
Birdy! Such a cool cat

always the Blues baby
Red hat lovely
oh lordy! all cheek! Obnoxious and jazzy
A racket and a hassle my girl!
My sweet dreaming girl

hair grease and hair spray
Lock to key
My woman and Me

Sketching from blankness all jams
are woken by this
grinchiness - the hipsters are eyeing us up and nosing her down
let's play some slang salad and
expose our age by our lingo

words always expose
So I'm white knuckle hand panting
the disclosure is in the bare quiet such no clothes and less
alphabet soup for the jacketed

later , after we revel
the world can get frosted
drive their cubes to Pleasantville

When the gas lifts
and we become visible to ourselves with each other again
I'ma write a drag racing burning flame sonnet
about you darling
just give me
a break I am bees knees lunging
into love Real Love -wrap warm jags together - get inside
from backseat bingo and take the wheel to love Such a whirl
for a writer !
my sour sweating pen paused all of the noisy applause,
gentlemen!

now i write madly and do not rhyme alone

with a sonnet and shimmy
dance hard , she does
my girl oh! her own woman
standing up for herself as
scribble does she beside me Unsweetly

pony tailing pretty a hive of many pulls -
our poetry is harmonious
and oh! her grammar
Good gods! riddles and
Real groovy curse words
cackle and pop
in a diary

I wish was a grimoire

Amy Christine Matus from Milwaukee, WI and WI Beat Poet Laureate 2019-2021, is a published writer and recently featured for G.A.S. Poetry Art and Music plus attends various events and festivals celebrating creativity.

Daniel McTaggart - Goodbye Is Still Too Soon

The earth above my father has been healed
For a few years now
Sometimes small flowers sprout
But mostly it's just grass
I only see a few small green patches
When I am not there
The patches hastily tamped by a shovel
Mostly I see loose ground still in throes of continental shift
I'm still not ready to see him completely buried
When I go by his grave
A baseball flies into my glove
A stack of comic books spreads like magician's cards
A rare coin is plucked from a jar of pennies
An ancient arrowhead is freed from layers of clay
I hugged my dad the morning he died
It's still too soon to stop
That dad smell still fills my nose
That mix of burnt whiskers and meat from
His favorite midnight sandwich
I still dream of him trying to tell me something
If I listen, he won't keep coming back
I'm not ready to hear
I'm not ready to wave
I want to catch that baseball
I want to read those comic books
I want to keep turning that coin in my hand

Daniel McTaggart is a working class poet from Morgantown, West Virginia who loves writing in diners and coffee shops. His poetry has been published in Kestrel, Backbone Mountain Review, and Amomancies. He has also published several books of poetry, notably "Midnight Muse in a Convenience Store" from Venetian Spider Press.

Joseph D. Milosch - 14 Lines to Night

Night, your sky is dark. Then, a speck,
the first star, appears. Then two — three
and you reveal the coexistence of light
and darkness. The moon covers its face
with the Earth's shadow. Its thin crescent
of light marks its location. While a band
of moonlight runs from shore to horizon,
the wind crosses the beach, and I stroll
on damp sand in front of the sea cliff.
Looking at your infinite sky, speckled
with light, I sing; and when I do my voice
extends an arm, and my breath is not mine.
It belongs to the wind, the ocean, the moon,
the stars, and the darkness between them.

Joseph D. Milosch has four books of prose and poetry. A Walk with Breast Cancer was selected for a San Diego City Library Local Poet Award. His book Homeplate Was the Heart & Other Stories was nominated for the American Book Award and the Eric Hoffer, Best Small Press Publication award.

Amanda R. Morningstar - An Ember's Lullaby

Orange and yellow shimmer back
in the lake; it could be beautiful
from a different angle.
Every night, she had the dream;
every night, her world was burning.
And then she was at school again,
Confusion's delusions.
And then she was in class again,
at her desk again,
was she in that dress again?
Remembering premonitions
as her world burns down around her.
It didn't feel like she had been sleeping:
"I had the dream again."
"But you're wearing the dress."
The hallway is full of echoes
as they all scream into the void.
She slams her locker shut
and the voices disappear.
She stares:
Alarm. Warning. Danger.
A call to action. A call to run away.
She waits in the office;
she waits for them to tell her it is all a dream.
"You can't go home."
They all refuse to say the words
as the world burns down around her.

Amanda R. Morningstar is a mental health counselor. She uses writing poetry as a way to share her perspectives and as a mean sense of catharsis. Morningstar finds solace in family, science, self-care, and jumping on the bed. She lives in Michigan with her husband, children, and bearded dragon.

Jared Morningstar - Blue Light Special

Attention, shoppers!
We'd like to direct
your attention to
multiple sales happening
RIGHT NOW
throughout the store!

In Clothing,
hundreds of styles
await you:
the same looks
all of your friends
are sporting;
the ones they
harassed you for
not purchasing
weeks ago.
Better late than never,
am I right?
Sure, they'll just call you
a Johnny-Come-Lately,
but at least you showed up.
We knew you would.

In Groceries,
be sure to stock up
on all of the new varieties
of Coke, Oreos,
frozen pizzas that
are better than delivery,
hot dogs endorsed by
the pro athlete de jour,
and don't forget the all new
Kraft Mac and Cheese/Cheetos collab
(let's make that stuff
even more orange)!
Just as unhealthy as before,
but, hey, produce doesn't come
in bright, colorful boxes.

That good-for-you stuff
isn't on sale anyway;
it never is.
Best to stock up on
comfort food,
and when you outgrow
those jeans,
just head on over
back to Clothing
to start spending money
on that new wardrobe.

And don't forget to visit Toys.
It's never too early to
start your holiday shopping
(see the Gardening Department
for our artificial
Christmas Tree in July sale!!);
this year's hot toys
are already available
to buy at an
insane 5% off,
and who doesn't want
to snag the new
Tickle-Me-Furby L.O.L. Surprise
for $95 instead of $100?
No one.
So, hurry up and get yours now,
supplies won't last,
we can't guarantee when
the next shipment is coming,
and you don't want Little Timmy
crying because Santa's magic
couldn't come through for him
on Christmas morning,
which is only five months away!!

And before you leave,
be sure to go over
to Sporting Goods;
those trendy new firearms,

the same ones promoted
by the GOP and NRA,
are ready for you
to take home today
to protect your loved ones.
You want to be a patriot;
we know you do.
Just be careful to
keep them separate from
those Christmas presents
that you bought over in Toys;
we won't be held liable
for anything that happens
at home… or elsewhere.

Thank you, shoppers;
we appreciate
your business and
we hope you enjoy
the products that you've
purchased from us
as much as we've
enjoyed purchasing you.
Come again soon;
we know you will.

Jared Morningstar is a high school English teacher and adjunct English professor. He writes about his interests and observations of the world around him. Morningstar lives in Michigan with his wife and children.

Jason Morphew - I lost a leaf

putting my earbuds in
sweet gum I think
from the graduation
trip to Yosemite
my daughter took
four nights in a tarp
with girlfriends
I lost it I have no
excuse I put it on the curb
and stepped on the leash
traffic rampant
blond mom staring
into the tree
above me where
my dog was looking
and I was worried
she would lunge
(dog not mom)
so I lifted the leash
and hurried on
listening to nonsense
already lost
but I had a leaf
from my daughter
I lost it
into the endless other
scattered pieces
of the world.

Jason Morphew is from Pike County, Arkansas. The Washington Post says his full-length collection dead boy is “presented with an edginess and sharp intelligence that makes the poems pop.” His second full-length collection of poems, Eject City, is forthcoming from Poets Wear Prada in September 2024. Morphew teaches at Stanford Online High School and lives with his family in Los Angeles.

Jacob R. Moses - Lottery

My mental health is a lottery
Stability is a daily game of chance

Unknown as to whether
This bingo cage will release
My exhausted survival skills
Or my self-destructive behavior

Eighty emotions contained in one heart
Six moods released from one brain

Shuffling like the wind
Inside a glass sphere

Sometimes spinning
Like a centrifuge

My precious energy is
Hyperactive and preparing
For an outburst
Of ear shattering screams

Too much pressure
To appear stable
After emotions
Are released

Every day is an act of gambling
Where I could experience
Combinations of simple emotions
Creating a complex
Inside a withered spirit

All these bouncing balls
Have the impact
Of my inner child
Jumping upon my back
Like an inflatable surface
At a birthday party

I’m getting too old
To appear stable to all
Who eventually get to know me

I do not fear violence from my enemies
I fear my mind far worse than any gangster

And my only supplemental number
Comes from the phone
From which I call the man
Who sells me weed

For sometimes
All it takes
To soothe me
Is a dime bag
And a lucid dream

Jacob R. Moses (AKA Jack M. Freedman) is a poet and spoken word artist from Staten Island, NY. He is the author of the full length poetry book, Grimoire (iiPublishing, 2021). In 2023, Jacob received an MA in English and Creative Writing from Southern New Hampshire University. Publications featuring his work span the globe.

MW Murphy - Shelter

You see them in the shelter. Faces pained
and strained.
You ask questions, sometimes they mumble
something in reply. More often
they are quite non-responsive,
nervously twisting stringy
hair or tapping incessantly
with long thin fingers on table
top or other palm. They look like
they could use a drink, they feel more like
they need another cigarette.
You hand out forms to fill out, they
begin to scratch hurriedly with
yellow # 2 pencils. They are more
comfortable with forms, with
written answers, than with words
spoken aloud, with secrecy
and stealth.
You wonder why they stayed
so long…

The heart trusts
long after the mind has
rationalized the searing
anger away into
  soft white rafts
  of steam
and the
  scabs have dried
  bloodied and crusted
  off, until only faint
  fading pink
  marks remain
  on the soft round arms
    and forehead (hidden
     by waves of hair)
and the black and
  purplish
  blue

of dented
shins
has melted
into lighter hues
of pale
baby blue
and tinted grey
and finger prints
of gripping (tight-knuckled) hand
on slender wrist
have leveled out
from deep dimples
into shallow dents
of hurt.

The heart trusts
and remembers
the good times
the warm safe
embrace
of shelter
and protection
that comes
with a good love
and
the early
days of
a bad one.

The heart trusts
sometimes too much
that is why
it hurts,
why it continues to
beat,
why women stay.

MW Murphy writes both fiction & poetry. She has a piece in the anthology Gathered Light (Three O' Clock Press, 2013), and a short story in the anthology A Shadow Map (CCM, 2017). Her work has appeared in two online poetry mags

"Breadcrumbs Magazine" (2019), and "Yes Poetry" (2020, 2021), and "We Are Beat" anthologies (2019, 2022, 2023). MW was a "featured poet" at the Rose Room (Webster, MA) this past May. She has done readings from her fiction & poetry at various events in bookstores, coffee houses, and parks.

Andrée Myers I Tell You About My Love Life, Part One

Do you know how they go?
– Frank Zappa

You send me a Zappa song
about Catholic girls with
mustaches and easy virtue,
and I think to myself, you don't know me,
but maybe you do, maybe it was
all written there on the sidewalk
when I'd go wrong direction
on the 10 rather than the 22
and end up on the East Side
blistering the beat in
saddle shoes and little anklets
looking past the formstone and the shadows
and whatever was on sale at Epsteins
to something my father didn't want me to see
but I saw it anyway.
I watched a priest get drunk that year
and in the summer,
made love to a boy I liked
on sweaty Sesame Street sheets
on his single bed.
So, no disrespect to Zappa, but
when you go back to seventy-nine,
think of me as Billy Joel's
Catholic girl, tangled brunette,
forgetting the stained glass curtain
and all the vows,
looking for the new.

Andrée Myers is a writing instructor at SUNY Cortland in upstate New York. Her poems, fiction, and memoir pieces have appeared in numerous publications, most recently in the anthology A Lovely Place, A Fighter, a Charmer. She's loved the Beats ever since she first read Diane di Prima'sMemoirs of a Beatnik. Originally from Baltimore, much of her writing is influenced by that city's weirdness. She is married to the poet Burt Myers and lives in Binghamton NY.

Ron Myers - At the Tobacconist
(For Neeli Cherkovski)

Your's was a moveable court,
a floating poetic residency
making every public chair a throne
no matter where our wanderings
led us around the Franciscan Terrain.

Even in this last all-male bastion
down on the southern peninsula—
obscured by veils of surrealist pipe smoke
and intermingled pungencies—
somehow the local fraternity know
you are a powerful magician
of some unknown realm.

Not even the practiced fervor
of the football announcer—
shouting to the back of your wild hair
from the hi-definition jumbo TV—
disturbs your faraway eyes while
"a thousand dreams within gently burn."1

Who knew you would leave so suddenly
like those ephemeral puffs of smoke,
my beat companion for flâneuring
interrupted?

—San Francisco, 2024

1 Arthur Rimbaud

Ron Myers wrote his first poems at Indiana University in the 1970s. In San Francisco, Ron has workshopped his poems with Harold Norse, Neeli Cherkovski and Clive Matson. His subjects include environmental causes, ancient world cultures, geography (exterior/interior), and love and its frustrations. His poems have appeared in Beatdom, The Brooklyn Rail and over a dozen anthologies in the U.S., England, France and Italy.

Elaine Nadal - I Gave You More Than a Symphony

I released the butterflies from my stomach
and allowed them to fly and search for gardens
and jasmine flowers in your eyes--
I saw desire. I gave you my rhythm,
my movements, my seasons--
loved you hard. Let you love me rough,
knowing what love could do.
Love made Dad abuse Mom. Love made Mom stay.
I gave you more than a symphony.
I gave you my imagination,
the ink to write a future we didn't have.
And like Mother, I stayed because I invested so much--
because I didn't want to let go of your hold, your scent,
the passion in your kiss.
But in bed, during the nights when the moon undressed
and hid part of herself, I wanted to hide too--
and I missed my music.
And I wanted to create other symphonies--
con gusto, dolente, espressivo, appasionato,
misterioso, energico, feroce--
because love isn't enough, and I deserve more.

Elaine Nadal is a Pushcart Prize and Best of the Net-nominee, and is the author of two poetry chapbooks. Her fiction and poetry have appeared in several journals and anthologies. Nadal has shared her work at many venues. She also delivered a TEDx talk on hope, poetry, and music.

Ben Nardolilli - The Eternal Offramp

Gas and pine, sand and salt abound,
nothing is abandoned, all is busy flying right on by

over the land and by the water
I let the wheels do the running for me though not to flee

as temporary captain in a driving sweat,
the vessel is minor and I have no hat to put out and catch

anyone who wants to share the blur,
or come along to make quick shadows for the journey

but no time to be lonely in a church of one,
I take in the incense of the region as it turns to a stream

with a highway to devour and shed,
I produce distance, with no need to ask where everyone is

Ben Nardolilli is a MFA candidate at Long Island University. His work has appeared in Perigee Magazine, Door Is a Jar, The Delmarva Review, Red Fez, The Oklahoma Review, Quail Bell Magazine, and Slab. Follow his publishing journey at mirrorsponge.blogspot.com.

Melanie Neads - Howl
(Univocal New York School Poem)

Oh God. Oh God.
Sorry for loss of words. Howl! Forgot words. Forgot words.
Yoko Ono's songs no comfort now.
Don't worry, don't worry, only for Kyoko.

Snoop dog got blow from cop.
J-Lo got crotch spots 'n' mono from Hollywood Bowl show.
Mythology of Hollywood. Howl.
Howl. God don't know, God don't know. How?

God don't know Don. Don don't know God. Howl.
Symphony of dystrophy
Poor folks loot shops
Irons, tools, tongs, spoons, stools, clocks
Stop!
Don't shoot, don't shoot
Howl. God nor Don
No comfort for poor (God won't stop wolf from door).
Howl. Howl. No God, no God!

Don owns world, owns shops, owns schools, owns ports,
owns porn, owns stocks, own bookshops, own bombs.
God for posh boys not for poor.
Monsoons on poor.
Bolts doors of Oronoco. Bolts doors of Boston. Bolts doors
of Stony Brook.
Two o'clock. Noon.
Two dogs growl soon, soon. Blood moon of sorrow
Tomorrow?
Don got condom on, Knock. Knock.
Clowns show of cock. Oh God. Oh God.
Stop, God, stop! Snowdrops bloom on lost world.
Forty photos of tombs.
World's womb blown to Sodor.

Don says world too cold
Woodstock cooks
Too hot, God, too hot.

No good, God, no good.
Howl. Howl.

Melanie Neads is poet, playwright and tantric yoga teacher, whose play Drowning Aristotle won the City Life Best of Manchester play award. A SEN teacher, who fell in love with univocalic form, whilst retraining her brain after a stroke. Her collection Selkie Singing at the Passing Place [Flapjack Press, 2015], co-authored with Sarah Miller, was Best Collaborative Work runner-up at the Saboteur Awards 2015. Her community radio plays Dandelions and Jam Buttiesaired on Bolton FM, in 2023.

J. D. Nelson - chalk outline of the sun

news con
troll

normal
ly+e

cause?
tick

J. D. Nelson's poetry is greatly influenced by the Beat writers, especially Jack Kerouac's spontaneous prose technique and the cut-up technique pioneered by William S. Burroughs. The English-language haiku of Gary Snyder and Kerouac have inspired his own work in the Japanese form. Nelson is the author of eleven print chapbooks and e-books of poetry, including purgatorio (wlovolw, 2024). His first full-length collection is in ghostly onehead (Post-Asemic Press, 2022). Visit his website, MadVerse.com, for more information and links to his published work. Nelson lives in Boulder, Colorado.

Marc Olmsted - JOURNEY TO PLANET MOOLAH

Vegas is a
reality show billionaire named Kylie regretting her implants
- an endless soundtrack of hyper music as I wait for my plane
Vegas is a miniature version of other cities waiting for
Godzilla
a big sign that says COMING SOON for a restaurant where I
wouldn't eat
- a glass booth gambling lounge where smoking is allowed
and a pink glow paints the Asian gambler's face a rotisserie
chicken
- much needed water is almost 6 bucks
and the desperate of all nations come here
to lose their shirts and fluids
in a zombie bet that ignorance will pay off with heaven
as I gather my wits for upcoming cheap travel's brutal ride
the body's endurance scrambling thought
with stretched out time & future cramped seats
in the terminal with nowhere to rest or hide

Marc Olmsted has appeared in City Lights Journal, New Directions in Prose & Poetry, New York Quarterly, The Outlaw Bible of American Poetry and a variety of small presses. He is the author of six collections of poetry, including What Use Am I a Hungry Ghost?, which has an introduction by Allen Ginsberg. Olmsted's 25 year relationship with Ginsberg is chronicled in his Beatdom Books memoir Don't Hesitate: Knowing Allen Ginsberg 1972-1997 - Letters and Recollections, available on Amazon.

John Chinaka Onyeche - Healing

To this artist who drew my mother's:
Fading portraits behind these walls made memories.
To the old thatched hut that is now in rubble,
& this old waterpot made of clay soil -
To him, I said: take it. Take my heart &
Etch within it the scars left after her death.
Take it. Take my heart &
Engrave on its vessel lines.
Here is a boy child swimming in ache.
Against a tide in a spousal canvas,
Perspiring hides & seek of a prey & predator.
It is morning. It is morning again.
Take it. Take my heart & heal it.
Heal it from this ache made from ill ties,
& heal it from words made sword-tacked
On the flesh of a tender heart through the ear.

John Chinaka Onyeche is a Nigerian writer of colour (BIPOC) and historian from Etche in Rivers State. He is dedicated to ensuring that the full scope of history is accurately represented. His writing can be found in various journals, including McNeese University, Tilted House Journal, and Brittle Paper. Connect with him on Twitter @ Apostlejohnchin.

Chryssavgi Kapella Papadimitriou - Do not let the dream fade! (Translated by Chryssa Velissariou)

The tireless daughters of time, the seasons,
come and go, dance with reason,
passing the baton from one to another,
Seeking the world to alter.

They remain in their endless waltz,
changing the world, yet always from scratch.

The sun at dawn, the stars at night, and the sunsets don't stray,
Galloping in time's order, they do not change their way,
with the same frenzied steed, day after day.

In their mad, eternal dance, we lost what we had gained,
Sacred struggles and efforts were in vain.

Virtue, peace, and progress disappeared,
Violence and upheaval are now worshipped,
wars of interests, biochemicals, countless viruses, fear,
with new forms, the plagues of the pharaohs are here.

In Antarctica, the ice is melting,
people are starving and wandering,
in desolate lands home seekers are wavering.
There is no beneficent place to settle thriving.

Lilies, violets, and daffodils no longer bloom,
No more in the neighborhoods, colors faded, scents poor,
Markets full of tasteless, mutated goods.

The courtyard with the vine stands bare,
nightingales have broken their bonds; we now live in cages or nowhere.

The beauty of art is lost, El Greco, Praxiteles, and Phidias remain in museums,
Abstract art thrives, grace, and substance in mausoleums.
Eros no longer stays up all night,

his quiver's empty, no arrows in sight,
no lovers of Verona, no Isolde or Cleopatra stargazing.

Innocence and romance are lost, roles reversed,
New gender norms challenge what was once rehearsed,
The "winged" god is neglected,
unless he owns a lot of money and luxurious cars.

Chains of technology bind us to the chariot of slavery,
Robots, artificial intelligence, this is our bravery,
the path of virtue and justice lost; hearts in wickedness.

Oh God, may the spiritual compass not be lost
with morning's dew,
this is the dream that nourishes hope anew!

The earth is groaning from pollution, crying out for help,
its cry echoes far and wide, afraid,
angels' trumpets sound
you must be vigilant... or you will be LOST underground...

Chryssavgi Kapella Papadimitriou lives in Larissa, Greece, and writes for national newspapers and magazines. She has authored two collective and two personal books, and a short film script, winning multiple awards: 7 international, 7 global, 3 national, and 1 from the Cultural Olympic Truce at Delphi. Her works feature in prestigious libraries such as the National Library of Greece and New York University. She is a member of several literary and cultural associations, including the Int/nal Society of Greek Writers.

Carlo Parcelli - Aldini (an excerpt)

Blimey Cyril! Four fingers of Gordon's, lad,
Sure as it be said,
I just seen a bloke raised from the dead.
And in such a state I be,
A whiskey neat or ten
Need counsel me where ta begin.
George Forster, what the court say
Most cruel murdered his wife and daughter,
He, the bloke late hanged at Newgate,
Be taken from his place of slaughter
And laid upon a slab.
And this Aldini fella proper probe his face
Wif two bits a copper
What the dead man's jaw began ta twitch,
And one eye flew open and
He bore a frightful grimace.
What this Aldini, son of a bitch,
Rammed a rod
Hard up Ol' Georgie's ass,
And the stiff arched his back
And kicked his legs
And punched his fist
In the Deevil's own defiance.
And may god take me if I lie
But he knelt on the table
And let out a piteous cry,
The same what marched to the scaffold
Be so ashen and frail
A wail deep from the bowels
Of what could only be Hell;
I dare say you heard it in this very pub,
Didn' you now, miles away
If ya had a mind.
And then he spoke, and I say listen close,
For I be a Catholic man
Set in me apostolic ways.
But I'll cross meself and
Loose the tale for another cup,
As I be on the dole and swear

On me mother's grave
As I best recall this be
What Georgie said:
"Suren't me Jane and me wee one,
Louisa, be dead.
But not by my hand,
But Jane, for lack a prospect,
Their lives undone,
What two in the workhouse
Already be blood.
But in that moment
When my neck rake
And I roil at the rope;
When the irony abide as ya thrash
Against this mortal coil
You but hasten it loose,
And all goes dark
And I glimpse Hell,
Devil's and all, and
Don't I be back among the living
With a tale to tell.
But whevver it be god or man
What by such sensation show his hand
At Aldini's this day,
I will not say
As by a mere hangin'
And this force coursin' the prospect
Of fortune what come me way.
So I seek management,
A bloke what can read and cipher
So I not fritter me gift,
Spectacle it be
As part to a pint;
As I be slave to that need
And so with accounts not so keen,
If you know what I mean.
Mind Satan whispered in me ear,
Just as Aldini stuck his appliance up me rear,
Georgie tell all gathered
At this Italian's house
And the pub,

Hell be nothing to fear, he say
There be no lack a employ down here
Ushering the damned to and fro,
Stokin' the coals, stirring the stench
What ta bring up the smell;
No belly be full; no throat be quenched
Slimin' the walls of me illgotten hell.
What Dante's be god's finer grading of sin,
The damned be consigned to go
And for a brief moment
By the hand of Aldini's physick
Didn' I peek in?
And wouldn't you buggers
Pay a farthing to know."

Carlo Parcelli is a poet desperately clinging to life in the prime nuclear target, Washington DC. He has published 7 collections of poetry and is National & International Beat Poet Laureate for Maryland.

Susanna Peremartoni - Stages

I.
I switched from the tablet
to my iPhone.
I waved at a friend
I'd just added.
He is sitting on a race-car,
in a royal blue suit.
I'm sending virtual kisses
while rearranging
my wardrobe,
a shift from winter to spring.
My present is so fast now
yet it's constant and timeless.
I'm looking into the mirror,
putting make-up
on my distorted self,
and I'm not answering the phone,
because my body is a plane,
it may be in spin now,
and my soul is spinning
as it is ploughing its thunderous roads.
I'm losing myself in reality now.

II.
Next to me, blonde boys,
almost looking the same.
Greased hair, old imitations.
They are talking about fashion
with freakish fake girls
with black hair.
Some girls get on,
waddling, with holes in their
fishnet stockings.
Scary tattoos on their white skin.
All together, chatting
loudly, terrible.
They kiss the blonde,
shaved or almost shaved

Dean imitators, who
are following them with
a weary, hungover gaze.

III.
They get off.
The party is over.
They leave their scent behind
and some shiny magazines
on the seats.
No problem, maybe
someone will take them
at the terminus
to use them as blankets
in a dark corner
of a subway station
covering twisted,
distinctive smells.

Susanna Peremartoni lives in Hungary. Earlier she worked in Germany as a ceramic assistant for seven years. She had exhibitions in Helsinki and Vienna. Since 2016, several of her volumes have been published in Hungary. Published in Italian, Canadian, English, Austrian, American literary magazines and online newspapers.In 2018, she was the producer of a jazz poetry CD. Two CDs were released, in 2021 and in 2023 she published her own poems, she had serval photo exhibitions and podcasts.

Stasha Powell (aka Stasha Strange) - Fragments of Infinity

I believe a kaleidoscope is magic
turning and twisting our broken parts
into something so beautiful
you don't want to stop looking at it
One eye to the light
The other shut tight, in the dark
It takes this balance to see the masterpiece
that you are.

We are stardust
Shining beneath the sun
Twinkling beneath the moon
We dance on water
Standing on clouds that,
like a hot air balloon,
can carry us as far as our
imaginations can
Paint the picture with words
or hands or in the noise of our own minds
That's what I believe

Join me up there to dance
With the ancient stars
That up until now you were
only making wishes on
Take my hand
We'll travel to the brink
of comets and constellations
The stars inside of us
begging us to rise
to join our celestial friends
in celebration
Overlooking the Earth
and beyond her the
magnificent universe.

Stasha Powell (aka Stasha Strange) is an accomplished writer who draws inspiration from the untamed worlds found within books. Her literary prowess shines through her publications in prestigious outlets such as Poetic Reveries Magazine, Ohio Bards, an Anthology, New Beats Generation, Blossom, an Anthology, Setu Journal and Sidewalk Sanctuary her debut chapbook.. Connect with Stasha on her website: www.stashastrange.com.

c. Kerri Powers - Joni

As moths left the streetlight,
I traveled to distant globes in a dream to find her.
On a sailboat of sailboats,
we were positioned for sun and sea,
over the greenest, bluest waters,
where sirens stopped singing to hear her.
There were hopefuls and hipsters
arms waving to freedom songs -
on a beach full of Rosa Rugosa.

The island bells tolled,
high, and resonant on the mountain.
As the sky rolled over,
it dangled a single star.
Joni took the stage in a seraphim grin
and straw hat.
When she sang, “Songs are like tattoos,”
I knew that she knew -
music is the lifeblood.

c. Kerri Powers is a New England singer-songwriter, poet (Memoir Poetry), and visual artist from Central CT. Her songs have been featured in television and movie soundtracks and garnered her performances at the Telluride Folk Festival, Philadelphia Folk Festival, Newport Folk Festival, and more. She is working on her first chapbook of memoir poetry and resides in Canton with her husband and their dog, Rosie McGee.

RescuePoetix - Every Bone has a Story

Spread out through generational theoretic musings
spaces between lay vulnerable, untenable
Where does it begin?

Within flaws that make us human
the very marrow they bloom in
anchored by fear and doubt
sweet strumming of self

I see me as I am, flaws and all else
In my strength, I believe
in myself, I trust
in wisdom, I grow

The very blood that gives me life
relays the essence of who I am,
as I am, now and to be.
Each bone has a story

Sinews that twist and flex
give strength to what doesn't end
each one, it begins within
that peace we seek

Destined to tell our stories
for generations to come, compelled and lived
beautifully flawed from bone to marrow
each story set in bone

RescuePoetix is a self-taught bilingual, internationally published and performing poet, workshop facilitator, teaching artist and recording artist. She is twice honored Poet Laureate: The first Puerto Rican woman Poet Laureate of Jersey City, NJ (2020-2022) and State of New Jersey Beat Poet Laureate (2022-2024). As a globally published and performing poet, she has recorded poems to music, in English and Spanish in print, digital mediums, audio releases and video platforms. For more information, please visit: https://linktr.ee/rescuepoetix

Hema Ravi - LESSON FROM FARAWAY LAND...

Dame Washalot, Saucepan Man, what're you doing here?
Hey, Connie! that's something we've gotta ask.
Where is Bessie, Jo, Fanny? How did you climb up?
Simple! I just slipped in using Moon Face's slide.
D'you know, you can get trapped here?
Of course, I do! snorted Connie.
I don't wanna go to school. I ran away from home.
Jo and the others don't know I'm here.
And I beg you, please don't let them know.
What'll you do here? asked Watzisname.
Well! uh! I'd learn to wash, bake, do anything....
C'mon...let me give you lessons in washing.
Ouch! My back hurts...How'd you carry such loads?
Well, Well, it's a lil magical love, chirped Dame Washalot.
Can I try my hands at baking? Will Saucepan Man's mum
take me in? What's this gooey stuff? And this color?
Baking's not your cuppa, either; you've no patience.
The magic is you've to love your work, Saucepan Man
clattered.
Dame Slap rushed in and squeezed her tight --
hurry home this second, or I'll send you to Goblin Land.
Go to school - your teachers don't whack you,
which is why you're good-fo-nothin-not wanna-learn, eh?
Your tresses, attitude, and talk should be soft, listed Silky.
Connie rose, tidied her table, and got ready in no time.
Mum wondered: all hunky-dory, nothing topsy-turvy!!
She grinned from ear to ear – atop Connie's table lay Enid
Blyton's "THE MAGIC FARAWAY TREE."

Hema Ravi is a poet, author, reviewer, and editor of Efflorescence from Chennai, India. She has made contributions as an event organizer, independent researcher, and resource person for language development courses. She was the Communicative English Trainer for the 'SheVIL STEAM' initiative by IITM, empowering rural girls in December 2023, January, and April 2024.

Paul Richmond - That hasn't stopped us in the past

Let's be clear
It looks pretty hopeless
Why waste time
Beating around the bush
It looks pretty hopeless

That hasn't stopped us in the past

The lies are getting louder
It is harder to hear the truth
There is doubt
That we will recognize the truth
When we hear or see it
It looks pretty hopeless

That hasn't stopped us in the past

You point out the many reasons
To give up
I have seen the light
In their eyes
Fireflies in the darkness

The creative experience
Creating for each other
Through our art
Expressing our love for life
For our home planet earth

As wars rage on

Yes, it does look pretty hopeless

With each new day
We began again
Shining our light in our smiles
Yes, it does look pretty hopeless

That hasn't stopped us in the past

Each new generation
Each new attempt
Each new experiment
Feel the excitement
We are alive
We shine our light

It looks pretty hopeless

That hasn't stopped us in the past

Paul Richmond was awarded beat poet laureate three times: MA, National, and LifeTime from NBPF. He has performed nationally and internationally. He has been published in many journals, and anthologies, he is also a publisher of over 70 writers and has 7 books himself. He created Human Error Publishing and performs with "Do It Now" For more - www.humanerrorpublishing.com

April Ridge - Catwoman Has a Bitchin' Hot Flash in Her Patent Leather Catsuit

She flies through the air,
dark and mysterious,
her catsuit shining in the fading sunset.

Strangely enough, again,
she can't get that Bruce guy out of her head.

She turns to do another lap
of rooftop leaps around Gotham's business district.

Not seeking out Bruce's seventh floor penthouse consciously,
but there she goes again, doing acrobatic flips against his window,
hoping maybe he is changing into Batman for the evening.

Her face masked, but flustered,
she does a couple of impressive back flips and
then whips off her mask.

Her hair drenched,
she sighs and grabs a towel
from her well-worn leather fanny pack.

Menopause is no joker.
One of life's biggest riddles.

Catwoman wishes she had chosen
a more suitable-to-her-present-age
alter ego when she was a younger super villain.

Perhaps a mysterious fan-clad lady of the night.

Or maybe Batwoman. Yeah.

Maybe she could seduce Bruce and
convince him to live in tandem.
She could bring him over
to the dark side of the veil.

Batman and Batwoman,
happily ever after.

April Ridge lives in the expansive hopes and dreams of melancholy rescue cats. She thrives on strong coffee, and lives for danger. In the midst of Indiana pines, she follows her heart out to the horizon of reality and hopes never to return to the misty sands of the nightmarish 9 to 5. April aspires to beatseasonal depression with a well-carved stick, and to one day experience the splendor of the
Cucumber Magnolia tree in bloom.

Anamin Reveron & Nelson Villanueva-Martinez - Do You Hear My Tears? Do You Know My Cry?

I have traveled the world of uncertainty,
Of heated soil
I have felt my knees quiver of pain
Weakened from a journey that has no end

Memories incarcerated by the crimes of time
Shards of light dispersed; they were left behind
My soul yearns to revisit moments so fond
A scavenger hunt to claim- the divine
For merging the shards can take me beyond

Notions of yesteryears enchant a mystery whispered
by days gone weaving a tapestry of nostalgia,
where memories dance in the flickering light of recollection.

The past, shrouded in the mist of time, beckons with a sense of wonder and intrigue.
Each whispered tale and faded photograph
holds a key to unlock the secrets of an era long past,
inviting us to unravel the enigma of days gone by.

As we delve deeper into the labyrinth of history,
we discover that the past is not merely a collection of moments frozen in time, but a living breathing entity that continues to shape our present and future.

Embarking these notions of yesteryears, we embark on a journey of discovery, guided by the threads of mystery that bind us to the tapestry of time.

Anamin Reveron is a published poet, writer and Program Director at a local action agency. She currently holds the title of 2023-2024 Cultural Ambassador for the Puerto Rican Day Parade and Festival Waterbury, CT.
Nelson Villanueva-Martinez is a Program Director at a local Nonprofit. Master's candidate in Counseling and Human Services at Post University. His passions include holistic health, singing and writing.

Charles Rossiter - In Days of Old
(For a dear friend)

In high school we hung out
discussed laws of robotics
and went downtown to see
the world

In college we were partners in stupidity—
loud obnoxious, throwing up on lawns.
The night we tied Iggy to your roof
his curses roared
across your sleeping suburb.
Your parents said I
was a bad influence,
and my parents
thought the same of you.
We never made that trip
we planned to Frisco.

When we met in dc, you were leaning
on the hotel counter in a pose I'd seen
you wear in teenage poolrooms
It was a good day, walking around
comparing divorces.

Years later at our high school
reunion, like the trip that never happened,
we laughed at our younger selves
danced old dances with girls we'd forgotten,
sang old songs and promised
to do it again
but we never did.

Charles Rossiter, NEA Fellowship recipient and 5-time Pushcart nominee, has been published in Bennington Review, Paterson Literary Review, After Hours and more. Recent collections include The Night We Danced With the Raelettes, a memoir in poetry, All Over America: Road Poems, and Green Mountain Meditations, (all from FootHills Publishing). He's performed Nuyorican Poets Café; Green Mill, Chicago; Dodge Festival in NJ, Detroit Opera House and Chicago Blues Festival.

Christine Rousseau - Change Happens

Yellow, orange, red mottled
Leaves fall and swirl
With season's change

A trowel restless for winter's stillness
Pierces soil deep
Severs roots thoughtlessly
With intention

Scoops growth emerging young and energetic
Tucks and tamps plantlets beside
Perennials past prime
Half spent

Buds of possibility
Brown out
With season's change

Christine Rousseau zooms in on moments in life through her poetry and photography. Christine lives in Torrington, CT.

Jason Ryberg - Scenes From 39Th St., Pt. 1

The Poet with The Hole in His Throat
was busy soaking copies of Black Like Me
in gasoline, shouting I told you crackers
what I'd do the next time I saw one of these things!
And the Eastern Academic Elitist Poet
(from (eastern-most) Hoboken) was
attempting to set Tennyson's Charge Of
The Light Brigade to jaw harp, tone box and oboe.
And the ferocious Celtic / Valkyrie Poet
was feasting on the still-beating hearts
of all the fallen poets foolish enough
to have fallen for her Celtic siren song.
And God's Angry Poet was casting out
the undercover Homeland Security Man
with Lilies of the Field and various
lyrical incantations and the street preachers
were ladling snake oil from a fifty-gallon drum
while some faintly unwholesome character
claiming to be the latest incarnation of the Bodhisattva
was saying to everyone and anyone on the street
HEY, PULL MY FINGER! PULL MY FINGER!
And then the ten-thousand myriad archetypes
became strangely quiet and still, the stars all stopped,
momentarily, in their places and the angels
and demons ceased their square-dancing on the heads
of pins and ten-penny nails, everywhere.
And still the Lonely Backwoods Bukowski-
Wanna-Be Poet sat there in a dank sub-basement
corner of his imagination, mindlessly ringing
wind chimes made from throwing stars, winding
and re-winding the ancient mechanical cricket of his art.

Jason Ryberg is the author of eighteen books of poetry, six screenplays, and a few short stories. He is currently an artist-in-residence at both The Prospero Institute of Disquieted P/o/e/t/i/c/s and the Osage Arts Community, and is an editor and designer at Spartan Books. He lives part-time in Kansas City, MO and part-time somewhere in the Ozarks, near the Gasconade River.

Mark Saba - Dunkin' Doughnuts

The young man on crutches
gives up his place in line.
I hesitate to stand in one

or the other, wondering
about this self-selection process.
How will I know what I want?

To the left, a woman who may not
speak English presses the screen randomly
then looks around as if answers

will come flying in from afar.
Is it okay to ask for help?
To the right, a young woman in miniskirt

knows exactly what she wants.
She commands the screen as well as
every detail of her life.

Both finish, the immigrant looking
as if she's just committed a crime,
the young woman marching off

to the pickup station. My turn.
I search for a small black coffee
and breakfast sandwich, no cheese

while holding back the anxiety of this first
experience—I've never been here before
and not sure I'll ever be back.

Orders complete, we wait.
The man on crutches has left.
Held hostage by our stomachs

our destinies lie in the hands of the order
takers. To them we are all equal
and yes, they often make mistakes.

Mark Saba's publications include Flowers in the Dark (poetry), Calling the Names (poetry), Two Novellas: A Luke of All Ages / Fire and Ice, and Ghost Tracks: Stories of Pittsburgh Past. His work has appeared widely in literary magazines around the U.S. and abroad. He is also a painter, and recently retired from Yale University as a medical illustrator and graphic designer. Please see marksabawriter.com.

Sarah Sarai - Summer on Mars

the all night
we rolled
and hot like,
slope,
hissing
yes yes
hissing
please always
thump elbow
and up and laugh
all over again
why not any
of us why
not now
I take you
we each and
you me

Sarah Sarai hit Route 66 when she was eight and her family relocated from New York to California. She is the author of Bright-Eyed (Poets Wear Prada), That Strapless Bra in Heaven (Kelsay Books), Geographies of Soul and Taffeta (Indolent Books), and The Future Is Happy (BlazeVOX). She received certification as anpsychic healer in Los Angeles in the 1970s.

Deborah C. Segal - Heretic Under a Left Hand Moon

Underground heretic hovering, covering clouds with twilight glimmering, chimera cowering, crossing over again, smelling a deep, dank aroma of glossy roses, rosy, rosy ring of poesy, red meaning crisis!

O, who is this giddy prince of darkness, O, little Peter in grease paint, O Juggalo!
Tell a giggle. And bells a-jingle.
The one-eyed Jack-O-Lantern laughing, doleful,
yet gleeful, chewing a twig, twisting bare arms, bearing the pleading, now hearing screaming, O, nameless creature of time, and woe!

A vole and a mole are emerging from a hole, and dancing in time to the porcine combo. Cloven and hard are these little hooves. First jumping to the left, then stepping to the right.

Throwing darts at the crescent moon, O, cruel moon, how your shadow draws down the last chord. Sepia sunset arrives to a crucial choir singing. Come to me, when you're weary, come to me, if you're hurting, I will try and lift your burden. Silver surfer sings. Come to me.

Deborah C. Segal lives and writes on the territory of Xučyun, the ancestral and unceded land of the Chochenyo Ohlone. Her publications: •□Edwin in the Embrace of Entropy, 2024, Another Seagull Productions •□Borderlands and Lines, 2019, Another Seagull Productions •□1975, 2019, MCTP •□Natalie's Story: A Raincheck for Jack Kerouac, 2013, MCTP

Toprak Shams - Lux Aeterna

They say that as it was in the beginning,
it will remain so,
The fathomless world, which was proven by
Shakespeare's ghost
through algebra over slow-limp dances

Thought is the thought of thought.

He walked over the waves, gave seeds.
If we win another such victory, we will be devastated.
The sky has turned blue, so there must be movement.
/Stop sulking.
In the pantomime of the great Turko
in the memory of the universe
I hear the devastation of space destroyed by
slander wings.

This lux aeterna is based on ages ago.

At the intersection of dream and reality,
We fall under the spell of these sentences.
What we feel in a poem,
It invites us to a journey towards eternity.

Couldn't
our
dreams
soar
a little

higher?

Toprak Shams is a poet & writer. His poems have been translated into Hindi and Persian; It has been published in various anthologies and journals in countries such as America, Germany, Nepal, Spain, Iran, England, Japan, Italy, Australia, France, Sweden, Canada, Poland and the Netherlands.

Ms. Til Kumari Sharma - Sea Light

Sea as the supreme source of sun light,
Universe is dancing with sea waves.
Thunderbolt from cloud and sun.
The horizon is dancing with nature.
The wind from the corner of sea.
The water as fire from the deep sea.
The desert stores sea light.
The sea boss to lead the universe alone,
The self-defense inside her is heroism.
Sea waves are weapons.
Conflicts within psyche of sea life,
Deep in breath, high sound of waves;
The power of sea life and herself;
The desire to kill human settlements;
Sea is dancing with the sea waves.
The beach of human settlements,
Tearing with immediate reaction;
Danger and struggle of sea light to defense
Eating many coffins
Giving life and essence together
Sea light is reaching to sun
To lead earth and universe together;
The existence of mine there.
Eternal epitaph of mine is composed.
Her glory of destructed art;
Her glory to have freedom to achieve.
Battlefield of nature & human in contrast;
Light and sun cloud with huge hailstone.
Sea light is my huge might with love.
Roaming as dancer to bring new civilization and leading source,
The shining arm of the oceanic beauty;
Blue in colors;
Fire from water;
The mysterious beauty of nature mother,
Calm sea with healthy life.
Often with mysteries disaster.
The sound in isolation with deep wound,
The medicine like light to rise me from ashes of my culture.

The huge orb of sea light with moral standard and historical face;
Sea light is in my inner wisdom.
New science should be alive.
Sun is mingling in sky.
Sea is leading to balance life for all.
I am searching the standard light of life.
My similar agony with sea waves
My similar wound within my life
The destructed love and fire in my eye.

Ms. Til Kumari Sharma as internationally recognized author is from Bhorle- Hile, Paiyun 7, Parbat, Gandaki, West Nepal. Her parents are Mr. Hari Prasad Basel / Bashyal Sharma (Mayor of Village Assembly) and Mrs. Lila Devi Bhusal/ Bashyal. She is featured-poet and best-selling co-author too. Her writings are published from many countries like Russia, France, America, England,Africa, Korea, Germany and many others. She is poet of World Record Book named HYPERPOEM. Her World Personality is published in Multi art 8 & 12 magazine from Argentina and Mexico.

Virginia Shreve - The Guest of Memory

He says his memory is so bad
but it is a matter of focus.
He remembers every line of her face.

He remembers the warmth of her hand
wrapped in his at Union Station
as he left to fight Hitler.
Were the cherry blossoms in bloom? Were there crowds?
Wide shouldered and wide lapelled, cocked fedoras,
crimson lipstick,
seams drawn down the backs of legs while silk stockings
parachuted the boys at Normandy?
Was there steam and grit, noise, steel shrieking on steel,
conductors' urgent bellow, and the acrid scent of diesel,
a sense of destiny and death?
He doesn't remember that, just her hand.

He remembers the feel of her hand
still clasped in his, fingers intertwined like roots,
five children later, sixty years later,
continents traveled, wars won and lost,
their youth on the Late Movie
and slumbering in forgotten addresses
forgotten place cards
Falls Church, Arlington, Pittsburgh, Nitro, Buffalo,
Golden Valley, Pompton Plains, next stop Kankakee

He doesn't remember the night of her Memorial Service
a chorus of owls
and the heavy beat of wings.

He doesn't remember Tybee Beach three days after
with oldest son and daughter, seagulls stalking the sandwiches,
a small girl on tiptoes flying a curtsying kite,
his words tumbling away in the wind

He remembers her laughter, like tiny birds bursting from a hedge.

He remembers her apple pie and how red shoes always made her happy.

He gives away everything

but her red shoes.

The crossword takes 12 minutes now, instead of seven.

His glasses go on field trips without him.

He remembers every line of her face.

Virginia Shreve is the Town of Canton, CT Poet Laureate, and was honored to be CT Beat Poet Laureate from 2020 to 2022. She lives in the small river town of Collinsville with husband and dogs, none well-trained, but all good-natured. Her poems have appeared in print and online in various journals and anthologies.

Jay Simpson - Survival

Music clings to bones mixes blood with water
paints abstract landscapes screaming seas
shadows nudge the loyal heartbeat
addiction survives on pretense
steals the end before the beginning
controls the willing corrupts truth
then the music stops
pennies drop from heaven
fall around broken umbrellas
click against cracked pavements
catch a hand a rooftop
a drooping flower a singular moment
a living breathing desire
possibility calls the night
jazz tunes intoxicate silence
weary strangers rest in thought
sunshine soothes the naked flesh
repels the blood the oil the dirt
wildflowers nestle close by
memories whisper weeping willows
intoxicated dancers spin in unison

Jay Simpson was born in Sydney, Australia and now lives in Perth Western Australia. She is recently published in Lothlorien Poetry Journal, Cajun Mutt Press and Alien Buddha Press. Jay is also the featured writer, both nationally and internationally in a number of online magazines and journals as well as other notable publications. Jay loves poetry, art, music, satire and black comedy. She is the Creative Director and Author at her blog 'Living Dangerously'.

Michael Sindler - damn good barbeque

we didn't drink
the Kool-Aid
but we drank a lot
of mushroom tea
and ate a lot
of damn
good barbeque
and ran laughing
through the streets
day and night we
danced and played
and fucked and drank
and slept wherever
the spirit beamed
and whenever
we careened
and all too often
with whoever
was in the other
half of the dream
we could have
built a house
from stems
and seeds
we could have
lived inside
harmonies
but too much
of a good thing
will always end
by crashing
in run-down
Victorians
and a long string
of shotgun shacks
making installations
out of knickknacks
and detritus

that led to lots
of nothing
which was perfect
when you think
about it
sometimes
even
making art
that literally
flew away
it might have
been nice to take
a picture but it
doesn't matter
anyway
it was all about
the moment
we let go

Michael Sindler, Denver resident, is the current Beat Poet Laureate of Colorado. He's appeared in various print and web publications and numerous anthologies including 2020: The Year America Changed, New Beat Poets, and Caesura. He has collaborated in a wide array of media bridging projects and performances and facilitated workshops virtually and in person across the globe.

Megha Sood - Act Beautifully

If only we could truly realize the consequences of our actions
preached endless times
but still failed to get the real essence.

If only we could hear the sounds of souls and withering
hearts
that we mercilessly shatter as we continue to live.

We live in a world laced with desire and hunger
of needs and wants, of acceptance and rejection.

While we continue to pave our path to success
no matter if it is laced
and seeped with the blood of many —we continue to live,
we continue to exist.

We look for monsters in others
failing to turn the mirror toward us
the faint remembrance of who we truly are.

Kindness that should flow through our veins
symphony of love that we all should syncopate to.

I'm lost here in translation. Like the tattered book forgotten
to be picked from the dusty shelf, old and forgotten,
waiting for
kindness that never returns.

And yet, here I am still waiting for mindless conversations
in this room to end slithering from one selfish ear to another.

Waiting for a sliver of golden silence. They say silence has its
own language
a lost art that needs an interpretation.

To have that stillness that lies in the knotted legs of a
meditative monk
or the mellifluous beauty of a swirling dervish.

To know that we all need to listen, not hear.
Listen to the heartbeats that tell us the simple truth.

To act beautifully, to find the plinth of our existence.
To find the soul of the poem open for interpretation.

Megha Sood is an award-winning Asian-American author, poet, editor, and literary activist from New Jersey. She is also a Literary Partner with "Life in Quarantine", at Stanford University. Her 850+ works have been widely featured in print, online journals, public exhibits, and anthologies. Find her at https://linktr.ee/meghasood

Belinda Subraman - Rainbow River

If we're reincarnated
Into the gravity of Earth
From the ethereal essence of One

We come back for the drama
We come back for concrete senses

Bouquets of pain
Bliss through the stars

We get tired of peace and Oneness
We come back for burning love

Belinda Subraman is editor and publisher of GAS: Poetry, Art and Music, an online zine and video show . She was recently named State of Texas Beat Poet Laureate (2023-2025) She lives in El Paso, Texas on the border of Mexico. Her latest book is Full Moon Midnight from Roadside Press

Kevin Patrick Sullivan - Touched

I read a poem today that made me think
how I came to poetry
the starry lit milky way
I always thought it was just because
I had a gift with language
the waves slapping again and again
the wind whispering
now I'm not so sure   maybe
poetry came into my life after
I went through that windshield
of a 1966 Pontiac Bonneville in the Autumn of 76
driving home after working all day washing dishes
then drinking all night celebrating the cook's 40'th
in Pismo Beach, almost home when I drove through that
telephone pole on Shell Beach Rd
the 101 at my back
after Spyglass Drive just flying through letters
towards the blue Pacific where I landed in a
field where the Cliffs Hotel is today
until the PG&E crews found me at day break
I had knocked out power to in the thick of night
points north all the way to Avila
I laid in Sierra Vista for days in and out of consciousness
Space
I had a five inch crack in my skull
not touched anywhere else
after the hospital stay the occasional blackouts
during the next year on Dilantin to prevent seizures
I started to pull words my mind and ear listening
my heart opened
                                        I did start to pay attention

Kevin Patrick Sullivan's has three books and a number of chapbooks. His poems are in SOLO, HUMMINGBIRD, ASKEW, LUMMOX, MIRAMAR, SPILLWAY, Madness and other journals. He Co-Founded, curated Corners of the Mouth at Linnaea's Café, a monthly of featured and open readings for 35 years, Co-editor of Corners of the Mouth A Celebration of Thirty Years a t the Annual San Luis Obispo Poetry Festival, Co-founder/ Curator of the Annual SLO Poetry Festival since 1984

Ashok Chakravarthy Tholana - To Restore A Perfect

Having pounded the surface and the sea,
Having punctured the land and the space,
Having destructed the deep dense forests,
Having encroached the high mountains;
We peeled the nature of its natural beauty.

We have devastated invaluable resources,
We have polluted even the life-giving air,
We have spoilt the pure water resources,
We have not spared the rare living species,
And peeled the nature of its natural resources.

We have infiltrated deep the green valleys,
We have played havoc with the rare birds,
We have hunted down the rarest creatures,
We have almost inflicted a terminal blow,
And peeled the nature of its natural elements.

Yet, with a perfect care and perfect concern,
With perfect action and a steadfast devotion,
Why not we act perfect, for a future perfect,
In a perfect way to restore a perfect world,
And bring back nature to its natural serenity.

Dr. Ashok Chakravarthy Tholana's message-oriented poems have been published in over hundred countries and the poet is conferred with several national and international awards, doctorates, commendations, titles etc. Apart, his poems have been translated to 40 languages as of now. With ten published poetry books, the poet has also translated 13 spiritual and 4 other general books from local Telugu language to English. He lives in India.

Igor Pop Trajkov - I Once Knew

I once knew what was good
there was simply no one to stop
something other than good
to develop in me.
You will say I was a child then
I had the bell jar around me
it didn't seem like everything around us
was relativized, so criminalized as well.

Back then everything was like the world
from the Disney cartoons was among
us, or rather like the good
Pluto extruded all evils.
Once then I knew how all should be
once then everything was fine
once then everything was with everything.
Then there was never a lack
of money, and therefore not of food and heating.
Once then life with laughter
was lasting, without much worrying
additionally preoccupying.
Once then I knew what was good and evil
very precisely and with that knowledge happily
I lived, only to find out later that there was no
good, but only evil; it's just that some evil
presented itself as good and so
I had to forget what is good and evil.
I now live with that ignorance and I don't even
know if this is how I want to live
for I must survive.

Igor Pop Trajkov is a renowned writer and film director from North Macedonia, multidisciplinary international artist as well; very prolific in all literary disciplines. Intellectualism, theory and activism are part of his rich agenda. He was published in some of the most significant magazines and journals; won few prizes for his achievements. His recently defended thesis in cultural studies is "The Culture Ambience of the South in Faulkner's Novels and their Film Adaptations."

Tammi J. Truax - At the Doctor's Office

In three seats lined along
the waiting room wall
they sit at either end
like antique bookends,
carved of despair.

A chair left between them
occupied by dead air,
a chasm that can't be filled
by anything, but the pall
of pain that hovers there.

In pristine librarian garb
she is statuesque, hard,
like a bird, slowly blinks.
He holds his own hand,
over outstretched legs.

Looking relaxed in all but
his contorted countenance.

Faded wedding bands their
only adornment, lie on each

gnarly old left hand.

I am afraid of them.

I am afraid for them.

What worries and sorries

have gripped them so?

Why now? And how

even with God's own grace

can this time be golden?

Tammi J. Truax is the former Maine Beat Poet Laureate and Portsmouth (NH) Poet Laureate. From a little house in the big woods, she works by day as a school librarian, and writes when the muse pays a visit to her humble hermitage. She has a funky fixation on alliteration. And rhyme. And elephants.

J R (Judy) Turek - Scribe

I am the words written on the backside corner
of your page, the doodles that are cuneiform
translations of geometric anomalies,
I am the scriptures written on sea crests
at Galilee, parts of prophesies written on grains
of sand on Iwo Jima, words spilt from countless
stones of sacrifice through millennium.

I am the love letters written and never sent
the unsigned Valentines never attested to
but saved in fifty years of dusty attic droppings,
I am the river of ink that floods the Euphrates
long before Gilgamesh rules his kingdom,
I am the storm of ink that swallows Atlantis
and I alone know the truth.

I am the keeper of alphabets strung together
to battle life and celebrate death in bloody verses
too long, too complex to commit to parchment
pages that would already have returned to dust
long before the letters of your name were invented
long before the stars breathed light, long before
I came to be.

I am the living memoirs of no-note suicides
of stillborn and smothered by dirty blanket babies
the scarlet letters shamed upon victimized breasts
the scroll of innocent women charred for witchcraft
for adultery, for fighting for the right to vote, I am
the numbers tattooed on forearms but never shown
never documented, never burned on a Maui beach.

I am the never-ending flow of ink, never-stopping pen
of injustices, the law of guilt to gavel precedence
over prejudice, the transcriber of death dictated to me
in sentences of 25 to life, I am the calligrapher
of dreams tinseled inside clouds, possessed
by syllables wrenched from a purple sunset,
the one who sweeps the floor for words you toss away,

I am the one
to tuck them in my inkwell
for someone more worthy.

J R (Judy) Turek, LIP&LR Poet-in-Residence 2024-2029, LI Poet of the Year 2019; editor, mentor, workshop leader, recipient of two pushcart nominations, recipient of the Conklin Prize for Poetry; author of 8 books of poetry. The Purple Poet has written a poem a day for over 20 years; she lives on Long Island with her soul-mate husband, Paul, her dogs, and her extraordinarily extensive shoe collection. msjevus@optonline.net

Tommy Twilite - The Promise of a Raindrop

I am but a single raindrop falling to earth.

My plan is to keep breathing for as long as I can, and then let go.

I will not live life feeling sorry for myself,
I will embrace sadness as part of the richness
of my experience
and move on.

I will know joy and laughter.

I will not give in to fear.
I will face fear directly and show courage.

I will forgive myself and learn from my mistakes.

I will love with an open heart, I will live in love.

I will forgive others and try to understand them,
but I will stand up for myself and my beliefs.

There are those whose hate and bitterness
will drag me down,
and I will pray for them but I will walk away.

I will stick up for those who are oppressed or treated unjustly.

I will strive every day to live life in the fullness of grace.

I will shine in the sun and all of us together
will make a rainbow.

I am but a single raindrop falling to earth.

Tommy Twilite is a Massachusetts troubadour who combines music, poetry, exploration and adventure into his performances. He is the co-founder and director of the Florence Poets Society and the host of the Twilite Poetry Pub on WXOJ Valley Free Radio. He is the editor of the Silkworm annual review, and served as the Massachusetts Beat Poet Laureate from 2021-2023. Tommy believes that song and story enlightens the Earth.

Karl Nicholas Urso - Empty Cup (for Audery. B)

It's time to grow up
it's time to grow up
no more waiting
to fill your empty cup
is it me
Or
is it your luck
to have something
in your empty cup
what is found
has not yet begun
yet love was around
before the earth begin to be spun
I want you to wake up
I want you to wake up
no more waiting for
someone to fill
what is your empty cup
is it me
or is it my luck
time has moved on
now you can't give a fuck
but what is with this empty cup
you will never know now
so just give up
where you are just some girl
he wanted to fuck
so just move on
now
and
let him find his luck
he already knows that only love
will fill his empty cup
And already gained
some of his life back
And
wished you good luck

Karl Nicholas Urso is a writer, artist, poet, and musician who performs locally at open mics and festivals around the Torrington and NW Connecticut area where he lives.

Chris Vannoy - Love dreams us

The stars gather around us
Smiling as they peep through my window
And find us wound in each other's arms
They sing songs of soft touching
Of lips and skin
They feel the wonder of two
Melded into one on this night with no moon.

So where will this trail lead us?
This trail of tangled limbs and melted Brie
Of unmade beds and confessions by candlelight
That spill undone
before the blue sky outside is cut with airplanes
Littered with palm fronds after a storm
We travel through neighborhoods
Ripe with post millennium futures
along the rocky shore of doubt
studded with hopes
of French toast and strawberries
Sprinkled with powdered sugar
with dreams of Paris snuggled warm between us

Chris Vannoy is an American poet based in San Diego, California. He is a member of a new generation of beat poets and has made significant contributions to the poetry scene.

Jon Veilleux - On a Ship in the Caribbean

Cuba glides by
In the hot Caribbean sun
While we sit
And read inconsequential novels
drink Perrier
And bake.
Revolution won
and
Revolution lost
Either way leads to the same conclusion
Peasants work
And
Never have enough
And
Rich don't work
And
Never have enough

Jon Veilleux is an escapee from the working world who has turned to writing in his later years.

Chryssa Velissariou - In Love's Twilight

I'm waiting for you to come
And let me know that you remember me.

Even though you've been by my side for so many years,
I still wait to realize
That I am not insignificant,
That I am not wrong
To insist on loving you
Despite our many differences,
Despite our unfulfilled desires.

I'm waiting for you to confirm
That what I give you is more important.
Tell me that I save you,
That your path back to me is your choice,
Even if we have sinned against each other's needs.
Tell me you don't blame me for your pain
So that I can forgive you.

Tell me that when you dream,
It's not to free yourself
From the cage of fear that enslaves you,
Tied hand and foot next to me.
Tell me that I managed to keep you
Because you are free—
Free to fly whenever you want or nest in my arms.

Tell me you trust me
Without probing the wounds of the past.

Chryssa Velissariou is a Greek poet known for "The Seasons of Love" (2012), "Momenta Aurantia" (2015), "Greek Crisis" (2019), and "100 Senryu Against WW3" (2022). Featured in over 50 international and 20 Greek anthologies, she has received numerous awards, including the World Poetry Canada and International Peace Ambassador Medal, the National Beat Poetry Foundation lifetime award, and the Poets Network & Exchange Award, recognizing her contributions to poetry and education.

Merritt Walden - The sacrifice__for Neeli Cherkovski

Crashing mind
Descends from lofty
Climb

Wildly landing against loam
The crackling bone
Dreaming wanderers
The howling blue dog star
Of yore
As we begin the adventure
Of lore

See the dancers
Mute sirens hypnotizing
These eyes with careless
Passionate gyrations
Pirouettes

Leaps spins
bows

Offering the joyful
Sacrifice of bodies
To an eternal

Idea

Merritt Walden was born in Madison, Indiana in 1974. He has been published in several print and online publications Nationally & internationally. Has 3 books of poetry published. He lives in Austin, Indiana.

George Wallace - Woman Of Mine Woman I have Never Known

Woman of mine woman I have never known, you are as smooth as you are brown-eyed, you are sad as a setting sun (other times sugarbright as a magnet), I carry your image closer to my breast than a bounty hunter or a missionary with his cross of gold (I cross myself in black and white); and if canyons laugh and echo my pain I also laugh;

and if it makes mountain goats uneasy I will tell them your name anyway (and search across lifetimes for you); for you are in shadow where women hide, and in plain sight, and you are in the cantina where rough men go to avoid the anger in my eyes; this is what it means to love you, like few before me ever could,

until long after I have passed on from this place,
to far greener pastures than these.

George Wallace is writer in residence at the Walt Whitman Birthplace, author of 41 chapbooks of poetry, and a Lifetime Beat Poet Laureate. He travels regularly to share his work with the world poetry community.

Jeff Weddle - The Secret

It's all there in the diary,
but of course
you don't know the girl who wrote it,
never heard of her.
You don't know the town
where she was despised
or the lonely boy who thought of her often,
even as an old man, long after her death.
It's all there in the diary,
but the diary was lost in a well years ago,
dropped in by the girl's hateful sister.
The confessions and fears,
the staggering truths,
the hopes, the dreams.
The delicate poetry of the angelic lonesome.
It's all there, mixed with the water
and the water is mixed with everyone
who drinks from the well.
Seek it out, if you can.
Perhaps her name was Sarah
and maybe she was beautiful.
It's all there in the diary,
but the diary cannot be reached.
Close your eyes and conjure her.
It's all there in the darkness inside you.

Jeff Weddle is the author of more than a dozen books of poetry and prose. He won the Eudora Welty Prize for Bohemian New Orleans: The Story of the Outsider and Loujon Press (University Press of Mississippi, 2007). His work has appeared in Albanian and Spanish translation. Jeff teaches in the School of Library and Information Studies at the University of Alabama.

Lynn White - Bluebird

I pretend to myself
that he wants to leave
and that I'm powerful enough
and ruthless enough
to make him stay,
to make him want to stay
and sing me to sleep
and sing me awake
and go for a flutter
if he wants to.
But mostly he doesn't want to.
He wants to Buk the trend
and stay here
in my heart
living
like a secret.

Lynn White lives in north Wales. Her work is influenced by issues of social justice and events, places and people she has known or imagined. She is especially interested in exploring the boundaries of dream, fantasy and reality. She was shortlisted in the Theatre Cloud 'War Poetry for Today' competition and has been nominated for a Pushcart Prize, Best of the Net and a Rhysling Award. Find Lynn at: https://lynnwhitepoetry.blogspot.com and https://www.facebook.com/Lynn-White-Poetry-1603675983213077/

Ron Whitehead - The Mysteries of This World

Nobody knows for sure how many people
have lived and died on this planet
since the beginning, or who the first
humans were or how they arrived
or where they came from.
Great civilizations, known and unknown,
have been born and, in time, died,
and are buried under deserts and oceans.
The mysteries of this world are what
have always intrigued me the most.
8.1 billion of us live now
on this blue green planet.
Overpopulation, migration, pollution,
climate change, greed, war.
How much longer will we last?
Other species have disappeared.
Great civilizations are long gone.
All my limited calculable evidence suggests
that the total number of human beings
now living will soon be diminished dramatically,
perhaps even to the end of human life on earth.
In other words, zero. We all be gone soon.
So why wonder about and ponder the mysteries?
Why worry about the unanswered questions
like what is the precise number of humans
born and dead since the beginning of time
and how many civilizations have vanished
that we don't have one iota of information on?
Lordy the questions I have are endless.
They go on and on and on. I was born curious.
But knowing that my time here is limited,
and the number of my days decreases daily,
every morning I ask myself the questions,
What will I do with the limited time
I have remaining? And how do I prefer to die?
Well, not in a hospital. I prefer to die at home,
or in the woods, or on stage, having fun.
Hand in hand, arm in arm, with Jinn.
I want to die with peace in my heart,

knowing I have done all I can
to uplift and inspire, to comfort and heal,
and to awaken anyone and everyone I can
to the fact that we all have a non-stop river
of creative fire flowing through us
and we've got to do all we can to keep
our creative fires burning. Keep the flame alive.
When one of us is lifted up we are all lifted up.
Eye to eye, shoulder to shoulder, we are all in this together.

Ron Whitehead, U.S. National Lifetime Beat Poet Laureate is the author of 30 books and 40 albums. The new OUTLAW POET: The Legend of Ron Whitehead feature length documentary is now available for streaming on Amazon Prime Films Documentaries.

Linda Bratcher Wlodyka - We Pivot

We pivot, scrape the scarred pavement
not the same as scoring one's initials in a tree's
bark or spraying graffiti on buildings; instead
imprinting words in wet beach sand.

High tide's undertow washes message away.
Mermaids camouflage amidst kelp and coral
while conches and octopi co-exist squid send
out their identity as an ink stain; once dispersed
only clear water remains.

We pivot, scrape the grass and dandelion
leaves under our soles as if shoes mattered at all -
our footprints like initials whittled in wood become
weathered, smoothed - over time our identities fade away.

At the end of our days what we did say is history
like the shards from an ancient bowl dusty
yet preserved in the earth's layers; leaves us left
to wonder who has supped from its remains.

Poets will shed their dripping tears, their beliefs on paper
akin to ancient hieroglyphics. What is there to say when
we fear our message will become dormant? Will we lie
down, turn eyes to sky and embrace the final pivot?

Linda Bratcher Wlodyka is the Massachusetts, Beat Poet Laureate, 2023-2025 and resides in Berkshire County MA. If Brambles Were Bookends Collected Poems, is Linda's first full length poetry collection published in 2023 by Human Error Publishing. She has self-published 3 chapbooks. Linda's poetry can best be described as emotive, quirky and her themes often celebrate poetry and poets.

Ok **umut yalim - anti-poetry n.1**

comfy
tree
walkin'
sunday
water
red x 31
elvis
kağıt (turkish word "paper")
decline
queer
lying down
knife
table
green
body
blood x 22
loving you
shake & rattle & roll
earth
dying
cold
old
london

a poem about two hitmen who meet
each other on a rainy morning in lon
donand begin a queer love affair in or
der not to kill each other.

umut yalim born in istanbul, 1984. he executes
anti-poetry since 2018.

Hiromi Yoshida - Beatitude
(about Gary Snyder)

Conjuring a living ghost
by G-mail, unbroken beat—
the phoenix unscathed by fire,
immaculate survival—
combing the grey-haired archive
for elusive answers—

I longed so much to press the question
about Gregory Corso's letters, but
dared not tax the silver flame
flickering within him, the cruelest
April of ephemeral snow,
National Poetry Month 2018.

Surviving Beat poet in our benighted America,
who lured long-haired crowds
sweating accolades—
overflowing the Ellis Library plaza
before the Alma Mater statue at Columbia University—
crumbling mummy in mimetic
time capsules, dissolving to manageable dimensions
electronically—
after Ginsberg, Kerouac, Burroughs, et al.
he remains

the fiery ash
holy relic of Beat fetishists
kissing the sky's sacrosanct skirts—
jeweled hermaphrodites
poised on the archived edge
of papered oblivion;
decaying golden tooth of knowledge
the unblinking sphinx
arthritic Zen hand
waiting for the postcoital thunderclap.

Hiromi Yoshida

Author of one full-length poetry collection and four poetry chapbooks, Hiromi Yoshida is a finalist for the New Women's Voices Poetry Prize, and a semifinalist for the Gerald Cable Book Award. While serving as a poetry reader for Flying Island Journal, she coordinates the Last Sunday Poetry reading series for the Writers Guild at Bloomington.

Aprilia Zank - high way

the highway stretches out
unequivocally straight, flawless
a shooting star
falling back to the sky

the dual carriageway shows off
three lanes in each direction,
high-performance, grade-separated
junctions for a non-disrupted traffic flow

traffic signs align like parading soldiers
mandatory, danger warning
cautioning about prohibitions
within intricate security-claiming conventions

beyond the highway, on the other side
sunbeams debunk incidentally
the inscrutable towers of the factory where
day in day out shells emerge from the assembly line

Dr. Aprilia Zank is a poet, translator, editor and lecturer in Creative Writing and Translation from Germany. She writes verse in English and German, and was awarded prizes at the "Vera Piller" Poetry Contest, Switzerland, and the Twowolvz Press Poetry Chapbook Contest, Great Britain. Her recent poetry collections are BAREFOOT TO ARCADIA (2018), and READING THE SIGNS, (2019). In 2018, Aprilia was awarded the title "Dr. Aprilia Zank – Germany Beat Poet Laureate – Lifetime", by the National Beat Poetry Foundation (USA).

Su Zi - present tense

i dream i don't dream i don't want to

heavily painted white siding
a yard of flowering trees
the cat has a creamy mane,
opens his mouth wide
too wide

the universe blinks

2
there is a circular travel bag
in olive pleather
set upon pale travertine
grimed with a century of transience
under public lighting

3
what is awake?
the sound of water
a crane calling past the trees
awareness of the air and distance

4
Momma's house had windows at the front
a column of light
solid-core door
midcentury cathedral ceiling
floating stairs

walk down to door
out the window,
past screening shrubbery
in the dark
to the left
up the hill
headlights
they're coming fast
i can feel them

darker in the night
with malevolence
i can feel them
and the light says yes
because they cross
(present tense 2)

garden prize yard
right for this glass
me watching them come
i yell
call 911 to those
above and behind me
call 911

and sit up in the dark
the cats in elevation
a voice at the
ear that hears still
a bit
shh shh shh shh

you mean that?

Su Zi is a poet-writer, equestrian, EIC of the ecofeminist, artist-book, poetry series Red Mare. Recent anthology publications include One Hundred Thousand Poets for Change, Border Beats, and the forthcoming Florida Bards. Recent titles include Flux (betweenthehighway 2024), and the forthcoming Danke (Ethel)

The National Beat Poetry Foundation, Inc.,

I founded the National Beat Poetry Foundation, Inc. to bring different perspectives to how people view the beat poets. I feel a great injustice was done in the past. My goal is to bring people together through poetry, art and music. Change the negative views and warped truths of beat poets into a positive image. I try to focus on the natural world, respect all forms of life, and help preserve what is left of the wild spaces and the Earth itself. We are all interconnected to each other. Our words matter. The beat laureates in my organization are trying to be better versions of themselves by doing good in this world. I'm building a new generation of beat poets. Freedom and growth and giving all people a voice. I did not experience that in traditional poetry circles. I wasn't accepted there. To me the word Beat means to keep evolving.

Debbie Tosun Kilday
Founder/Owner/Director
National Beat Poetry Foundation, Inc.
& It's Different Nat'l & Int'l Festivals

http://nationalbeatpoetryfoundation.org
Email - nbpf15@gmail.com

Find us on Facebook,

You Tube:
https://www.youtube.com/
@nationalbeatpoetryfoundati5845/videos

X@BeatPoetryFest)

Instagram (dtkbeatpoetnbpf)

Look for our publications:
New Generation Beat Publications
Online Magazine - BeatLife.org

Printed in Great Britain
by Amazon

46193892R00129